All Work Is Cultural Work

Inequality at Work

Perspectives on Race, Gender, Class, and Labor

Series Editors: Enobong Hannah Branch and Adia Harvey Wingfield

Inequality at Work: Perspectives on Race, Gender, Class, and Labor provides a platform for cultivating and disseminating scholarship that deepens our knowledge of the social understandings and implications of work, particularly scholarship that joins empirical investigations with social analysis, cultural critique, and historical perspectives. We are especially interested in books that center on the experiences of marginalized workers; that explore the mechanisms (e.g., state or organizational policy) that cause occupational inequality to grow and become entrenched over time; that show us how workers make sense of and articulate their constraints as well as resist them; and that have particular timeliness and/or social significance. Prospective topics might include books about migrant labor, rising economic insecurity, enduring gender inequality, public and private sector divisions, glass ceilings (gender limitations at work) and concrete walls (racial limitations at work), or racial/gender identity at work in the Black Lives Matter era.

Nikita Carney, *All Work Is Cultural Work: Diasporic Haitian Women, Paid Labor, and Cultural Citizenship*

Celeste Vaughan Curington, *Laboring in the Shadow of Empire: Race, Gender, and Care Work in Portugal*

Julie C. Keller, *Milking in the Shadows: Migrants and Mobility in America's Dairyland*

David C. Lane, *The Other End of the Needle: Continuity and Change among Tattoo Workers*

Annette Nierobisz and Dana Sawchuk, *American Idle: Late-Career Job Loss in a Neoliberal Era*

All Work Is Cultural Work

Diasporic Haitian Women, Paid Labor, and Cultural Citizenship

NIKITA CARNEY

Rutgers University Press
New Brunswick, Camden, and Newark, New Jersey
London and Oxford

Rutgers University Press is a department of Rutgers, The State University of New Jersey, one of the leading public research universities in the nation. By publishing worldwide, it furthers the University's mission of dedication to excellence in teaching, scholarship, research, and clinical care.

978-1-9788-2831-5 (cloth)
978-1-9788-2830-8 (paper)
978-1-9788-2832-2 (epub)

Cataloging-in-publication data is available from the Library of Congress.
LCCN 2025012714

A British Cataloging-in-Publication record for this book is available from the British Library.

References to internet websites (URLs) were accurate at the time of writing. Neither the author nor Rutgers University Press is responsible for URLs that may have expired or changed since the manuscript was prepared.

♾ The paper used in this publication meets the requirements of the American National Standard for Information Sciences—Permanence of Paper for Printed Library Materials, ANSI Z39.48-1992.

rutgersuniversitypress.org

To all of the Haitian women, including each and every woman who helped me with this study, who have made me the person I am today.

Contents

All Work Is Cultural Work

Introduction

"Piti, piti, wazo fe nich li." The proverb is one of my favorites. I have had it pinned up in my workspaces for over a decade since I first learned it from a mentor in a Haitian Kreyòl language class I took as an adult in Boston, Massachusetts. This was an effort on my part to claim, or perhaps reclaim, the Haitian part of my ancestry, as my Haitian mother never taught me or my brother so much as a word of Kreyòl. She speaks it fluently, and frequently, with her siblings, and she spoke it with her parents as well before they passed.

And yet, my mother recalls this proverb in French, not in Haitian Kreyòl. She grew up as a member of the Haitian bourgeoisie and is proud of her command of the French language: "Petit à petit, l'oiseau fait son niche." In English it means "Little by little, the bird builds its nest." I have used it as inspiration to keep chipping away at whatever project sat before me, knowing that no matter how large the task, it could be completed bit by bit. But now the proverb takes on a different meaning for me as well.

I called my mom while writing this introduction to ask her about the proverb and what it means to her. She replied that it means building a life, little by little, or moving forward in life. I now see it as it related to women undertaking the daunting and seismic task of moving to a new country and building homes for themselves and their families. In the context of this study, this proverb means working toward cultural citizenship and belonging step by step, just as my grandmother and mother did, and just as the women in this book have done.

Given current anxieties over immigration in North America and Europe, questions of who belongs within the nation remain as relevant and pressing now as ever. Indeed, as I interviewed Haitian migrant women in Boston, Montreal, and Paris, I found that they, too, had felt similar tensions around belonging within their new national contexts upon migration. Each of these women carved out a place for themselves within the nation through cultural work, often in the form of paid labor. Through that work they built their new homes, bit by bit, just as the resilient bird in the opening proverb.

In *All Work Is Cultural Work,* I focus in on the lived experiences of Haitian women in diaspora to understand larger processes of belonging and inclusion in the United States, Canada, and France. This research project is a multisited, transnational study that examines how migrant Haitian women negotiate cultural citizenship and national belonging through their relationships to the paid workforce. Focusing on the experiences of Black (by Western standards) immigrant women, this research will demonstrate the ways in which gender, race, culture, and nation are mutually constitutive categories that are constantly challenged and investigate the conflicts and contradictions that arise around citizenship and national identity.[1] I seek to uncover the historical, economic, and cultural processes that determine conditional inclusion or exclusion of migrants from various nations.

Through this work on cultural citizenship, I aim to (1) extend dominant theories of national belonging, placing these theories in the intersectional context of transnational gendered networks; (2) provide a gender-specific analysis of the processes of migration, labor, and national belonging for Haitian women in diaspora, as gender is uniquely suited to amplify and augment the aspects of migration, labor, and national belonging that tend to be in the background when these factors are all studied separately; and (3) center the experiences of Haitian women and draw on the knowledge that emanates from their survival strategies, highlighting the ways that their particular positioning at the interstices of race, gender, labor, and migration illustrate the complex developments at play for migrants. The role of paid labor and the global political economy remain central throughout my analysis.

Grounded in ethnographic research with Haitian women in Boston, Montreal, and Paris, I use a transnational approach to query the putatively fixed categories of "nation" or "nation-state."[2] Using the theory of "transnationalism from below," I seek to unpack transnational processes of migration and citizenship, illustrating the micro-sites of power where notions of citizenship and nationhood are constantly constructed and reconstructed.[3]

This project sets out to address the following questions:

- How do work, race, gender, and class figure into national belonging for Black women immigrants?
- What role does paid labor play in negotiating racial and ethnic hierarchies within various nations for Haitian women in diaspora?

- What can the critical marginality of Haitian women in diaspora tell us about processes of belonging within various nations?

In addition to providing broader historical context to Haitian women's experiences in each field site, I take paid labor as a site of inquiry, examining the ways in which race, class, and labor intersect in the lives of Haitian transmigrants and influence constructions of racial and ethnic identity for migrants and the greater community.[4] Looking specifically at paid labor ties experiences of race and ethnicity to larger structures of the global political economy. Neoliberalism, like race and ethnicity, transcends national borders but unfolds in particular ways in particular places as it is shaped by the local historical context. Simultaneously, this multisited study illuminates ways in which the relationships between and among sites shape expressions of race and ethnicity for Haitian women.

Why examine paid labor to uncover processes of national belonging and inclusion? I assert that paid work outside the home interpellates Haitian women into a complex kind of national consciousness through which Haitianness is remade in dialogue with other national contexts.[5] Looking specifically at paid labor establishes a connection between experiences of national belonging and larger structures of the global political economy. This project examines national belonging as a form of cultural citizenship; I define the latter as processes of belonging and acceptance, a product of both self-making and subject-making, within a neoliberal state in which degrees of belonging are contingent upon one's race, ethnicity, gender, class, and relationship to the paid workforce.[6] Cultural citizenship is also a product of subjugation by capital, nation-states, and gendered structures of power. I use the terms "cultural citizenship" and "national belonging" interchangeably in this chapter, as I argue that cultural citizenship, contrary to traditional conceptions of citizenship, references the processes by which national belonging is negotiated and produced.

Haitian women in diaspora regularly engage in paid labor in their new national contexts, contributing economically and culturally to both Haiti and their new nation. I examine how Haitian women create and re-create multiple national contexts in the course of their paid labor, in order to extend current conceptualizations of cultural citizenship to include paid labor as an important site where cultural citizenship is forged and negotiated. In this book I consider paid labor as a locus of inquiry, examining the ways in which gender, migration, and labor intersect in the lives of Haitian women in diaspora, contributing to shaping their relationships to various nations. Through their paid labor, Haitian women negotiate their positioning within the nation by coming into contact with others within the nation in daily, micro-level interactions. I argue that paid labor is central to the concepts of cultural citizenship and national belonging.

Paid labor plays a crucial role in how Haitian women in diaspora negotiate living in multiple national contexts simultaneously. Even if Haitian women are dissatisfied with their placement in the labor hierarchy, paid labor abroad allows them to engage in daily interactions through which national identity and belonging are forged.

Cultural Work

Cultural work relates to citizenship in that it provides the labor that creates and maintains the nation. Cultural work is an act of cultural citizenship, demonstrating one's place within the national context, and a cultural worker is anyone who engages in the production and reproduction of the culture of a nation. Cultural work includes the work of artists and those typically recognized as producers of culture, but it also entails everyday social interactions through which culture is produced. Those everyday interactions shape the nation from the ground up through micro-level exchanges. I examine cultural work that takes place particularly in the context of paid labor outside the home.

Much scholarship on citizenship focuses on large structural forces of the state and the global political economy that shape the rules of national inclusion. In this top-down conceptualization, individuals have little power within these large structures. I build upon existing scholarship on cultural citizenship by using the concept of cultural workers to illustrate the ways in which Haitian women actively shape the nation through their paid labor, emphasizing bottom-up nation-making of Haiti and the other nations they inhabit and shifting the focus to examine both micro- and macro-level processes at play.

While engaging in cultural work and negotiating cultural citizenship, migration entailed shifts in class position and gender roles for Haitian immigrants. Many women, particularly in Boston and Montreal, expressed a desire to return to Haiti "someday" but had trouble envisioning a time when Haiti would be able to offer the security and relative comfort they experienced abroad. Particularly for Haitian migrants during the first wave of migration under the Duvalier dictatorship between 1957 and 1986, moving abroad meant a shift in gender roles that permitted Haitian women a level of economic independence they did not necessarily enjoy in Haiti. In this way, becoming economic citizens of nations abroad allows Haitian women to augment their participation economically in both Haitian and other national contexts. As Roseline, featured in chapter 4, stated, "Do you know what the most addictive thing in the world is? A paycheck."

I assert that workplace interactions shape national identity in the daily negotiation of cultural values, norms, and behaviors that indicate who belongs within various national contexts. I use the lens of cultural work to examine how specific examples of Haitian women's labor in each field site act as cultural work that creates and maintains multiple national contexts simultaneously. Next, I highlight how the political context of each field site shapes the expression of cultural work, particularly with regard to Haitian organizations and institutions abroad. Finally, using the ethnographic data provided, I make a theoretical argument about the necessity of reframing conceptions of cultural citizenship to include the centrality of paid labor. I intentionally foreground micro-level ethnographic data to illustrate the concept of cultural work as a strategy to counter dominant conceptions of citizenship as a structure that is imposed on individuals. The Haitian women I met negotiated the bounds of citizenship as active agents, not as passive objects of state power. That said, in order to fully appreciate the complexity of the processes at play, we must look at state and global forces alongside the creative strategies of individuals on the ground. These pieces together allow us to examine processes of labor, migration, and national belonging in a way that generates innovative ways of thinking about citizenship and national inclusion more broadly.

The concepts of cultural citizenship and cultural work ground my analysis by providing theoretical links between paid labor and national belonging. While other works reference connections between cultural citizenship and paid labor, this book brings together the threads to make a cohesive argument for cultural citizenship as involving paid labor, particularly for Haitian women immigrants but also for native-born and other immigrants in general. The multisited method allows us to see processes of cultural citizenship and paid labor as transnational processes that move beyond national borders while remaining rooted in the contexts of particular nations. The transnational approach is particularly clear in the case of immigrants who literally cross boundaries and have both economic and affective ties in multiple nations. However, understanding the concept of cultural citizenship as it intersects with paid labor in the context of Haitian immigrants allows us to understand that cultural citizenship and paid labor function transnationally more broadly. Cultural citizenship exists within and between multiple national contexts.

The case of the Haitian diaspora can greatly enrich conversations about processes of belonging within the nation by highlighting the intersections of race, gender, migration, and national inclusion in the lives of Haitian women engaged in paid work. Using an intersectional lens of analysis that centers race, gender, class, and place, I examine how gender roles shift upon migration, particularly in relation to work. We can learn much from the Haitian people dispersed around the world about the boundaries of citizenship and nations. Much of the mainstream literature on nations and citizenship works from a Western standpoint, grounding general theory in the particularities of Western European history. The richness of Haitians' lived experiences in diaspora can shed light on the complex processes of citizenship that may be difficult to examine from a dominant, white, male perspective at the center of the nation.

I engage with this mainstream theory to the extent that it is useful and then analyze the case study of the Haitian diaspora to challenge and extend existing theories of national belonging. I use the works of other scholars, particularly the literature regarding cultural citizenship, to support my departure from mainstream theories of national belonging and to interrogate current canonical understandings of nation and citizenship. This study links the particulars of daily life of Haitian women in each locale to the broader global political context within which these micro-level interactions occur, creating an analysis that connects the micro- and macro-level processes of migration and belonging.

Scholars of Haitian studies have documented the complex processes through which Haitians in diaspora organize around ethnic, racial, and national identity formations.[7] Schiller et al. insightfully draw a distinction between ethnic and national organizing, explaining that while the two are often conflated and sometimes occur simultaneously, they are in fact separate processes.[8] Given the scope of my project with field sites in three separate nation-states, plus Haiti as a nation that extends beyond the bounds of territory, I focus on ethnic and national organizing as overlapping processes. While I use the terms "nation-building" and "national context" for ease of communication, I very consciously view each nation and each diasporic "community" as multiple, diverse, and constantly in flux. As aptly summarized by several research participants in Montreal, there is no singular Haitian community in the city, but rather multiple Haitian communities. This conceptualization of nations and communities is necessarily messy and complex in order to reflect accurately the messy and numerous processes by which nations and communities are formed.

The complex histories of the women I spoke to for this study illustrate the need for a transnational analysis of Haitian women in diaspora. In some instances, their experiences highlight differences between field sites. In other instances, their experiences demonstrate that the field sites are inextricable from each other and cannot be studied in isolation. Migration trajectories of women in this study include Florida to Montreal, Montreal to Boston, New York to Paris, stints in the Middle East, sub-Saharan Africa, and other Caribbean islands, among others.

Though Haitian women of all walks of life emigrate from Haiti, the particular experiences that I seek to draw attention to are those of middle-class Haitian women. Pierrette Hondagneu-Sotelo highlights the fact that "most of the recent immigration research has focused on immigrant groups that are socioeconomically disadvantaged, those who have entered as labor migrants or political refugees."[9] This tendency for social scientists to study those of a lower socioeconomic status than themselves perhaps reflects issues of attaining access to other populations. For this reason, looking at middle-class Haitian immigrants contributes to the existing literature on gender and migration in a particularly useful way. Researching middle-class immigrants who have undergone several shifts in socioeconomic status upon moving abroad to "Western" nations and then integrating into their new host societies allows for unique insight into the processes of integration and belonging. As members of the middle and upper classes in Haiti, the women in this study almost universally experienced downward class mobility upon migration. The process of moving from a poor, Black nation to a "Western" nation leads to downward mobility for many who travel from the Global South to the Global North. In the case of Haitian women, however, many of them were able to gain middle-class status in their new societies after years of living and working in their new homes.

The jobs people hold provide them with incomes that place them in particular socioeconomic classes. Employment also connotes socially useful labor that can be claimed as justification for inclusion in the nation. This book, however, looks at work primarily as a site of interactive social and cultural practice, and at the workplace as a site where diasporic workers negotiate cultural inclusion and exclusion in the nation of arrival. Through this study I contribute to existing scholarship by analyzing the relationship between Haitian women, paid labor, and transnationalism.

I provide examples of social ties that embody social inclusion, exclusion, and what I term "complex inclusion" to illustrate the range of social relations that Haitian women experience in the workplace and how those relations differently situate Haitian women with regard to the nation. Complex inclusion entails the ways in which parts of social ties serve to include Haitian women, such as creating connections between others in the nation, but also how social ties can foster exclusion through forces of race, class, gender, and xenophobia that manifest in those social ties.

This introductory chapter first covers some of the literature on cultural citizenship, gender and migration, and transnational ties to lay the groundwork for the coming chapters, referencing and exploring additional literature as relevant. Next, this chapter provides an outline of the methods specific to this research project. Finally, it closes with an outline of the chapters that follow, providing a roadmap for the rest of the book.

Paid Labor and Cultural Citizenship

The term "citizenship" is generally defined as membership of or belonging to a nation or state.[10] Most scholarly definitions of citizenship revolve around the contours of legal and political citizenship, economic citizenship, or cultural citizenship.[11] In his work, sociologist T. H. Marshall identifies the civil, the political, and the social (or economic) as the three main elements that make up the concept of citizenship. He explores links between citizenship and labor, even contending that in some ways, citizenship depends on positioning inside the workforce.[12]

Scholars challenge Marshall's theory by arguing that his definition of citizenship focuses on a white, middle-class man as the imagined citizen subject and does not account for factors such as race and gender.[13] Through my analysis, I seek to examine cultural citizenship with a specific focus on race, gender, and migration, while keeping in mind how notions of citizenship, nation, and belonging are constantly in flux.

The findings of this study necessitate a rethinking of the term "cultural citizenship," as the experiences of the Haitian women I interacted with suggest a centrality of paid labor in establishing a sense of belonging within the nation. Scholarship on cultural citizenship emerged to capture the ways that social membership reaches beyond political and economic realms. Scholars typically identify cultural citizenship in terms of cultural belonging and acceptance.[14] For Nick Stevenson, cultural citizenship speaks to the increasing importance of knowledge and culture in shaping the definition of modern society.[15] For Aihwa Ong, cultural citizenship is about webs of power and subject-formation within the nation-state.[16] Ong also considers forms of cultural citizenship that take place in diaspora. While scholars do not necessarily agree on the exact definition of cultural citizenship, the term serves as a useful tool of analysis when examining issues of migration and inclusion or exclusion within the nation because it can serve as a placeholder for a multitude of social processes that link race, economy, and national belonging.

Culture weighs heavily in shaping perceptions of citizenship. An examination of cultural citizenship requires looking beyond obvious cultural practices of national belonging, such as national anthems or Independence Day celebrations, and instead looking at culture more broadly as the full range of symbolic practices in everyday life.[17] This project turns away from the sensational and the spectacular to investigate the ways in which daily practices shape cultural inclusion (and exclusion) in the nation. By employing the use of ethnographic fieldwork and in-depth interviews, I ground my theoretical contributions regarding cultural citizenship in the life stories and day-to-day experiences of Haitian women.

Concepts of belonging and inclusion in society serve as central to the notion of cultural citizenship. French scholar Jean Leca asserts, "Citizenship depends on . . . symbols of collective identification which are accepted by those who are 'still at the door.' These symbols must permit the latter group of newcomers to aspire to and attain the realization of the first two conditions, and to pay the 'cost of access' to the community."[18] The "cost of access" that Leca refers to here entails the oppression, marginalization, and stereotyping of recent migrants by previously established community members. This study examines the "cost of access" required of Haitian migrants by native-born (often white) citizens of the United States, Canada, and France. Issues of cultural inclusion are closely linked with notions of national identity, as amorphous and ever-changing as they may be. I argue that national identity is continuously constructed, always multiple and at times contradictory, and central to issues of cultural inclusion and exclusion.[19] For instance, Wideline in chapter 6 is actively participating as part of the nation in her job as a nursery school teacher, yet that job is a form of gendered and low-status labor that situates her within the nation in particular ways with regard to her race and gender.

Renato Rosaldo, Aihwa Ong, and others make a crucial contribution to studies of social membership, citizenship, and national identity through evidence and analysis that see lived experience as the crucible in which cultural citizenship is created.[20] Ong's work in particular is extremely relevant to this study in that she identifies polylateral and transnational relationships outside the nation of emigration as a continuing part of the life of the nation, complicating previous models of migration based on binaries between nation of departure and nation of arrival and encouraging a transnational theorization of cultural citizenship. Ong's definition of cultural citizenship complicates notions of belonging by identifying the role of an individual as well as the role of "webs of power" in citizen-making.

I draw heavily from Ong's definition of cultural citizenship, which remains deeply attentive to race, gender, and class. I argue that scholarship has much to gain by more fully examining the relationships among cultural citizenship, migration, and paid labor and that this study of the Haitian diaspora provides generative data to further explore this relationship. As in Karine's experiences in chapter 6, paid labor is central to her developing a sense of belonging within both the Haitian and Quebecois national contexts. Through her paid labor, she works to reproduce Haitian national culture abroad and contribute to Quebec's multicultural landscape, and in so doing, she creates a space for herself as a cultural citizen within Haiti and Quebec. Paid labor situates Karine within the context of the nation through cultural and economic exchanges. Karine's embodiment of cultural citizenship illustrates the ways in which citizenship is not only a top-down process but also a bottom-up process in which individuals work to shape their positioning and sense of belonging within the nation.

The state constructs citizens in specific ways, such as their roles or identities as taxpayers, workers, consumers, and welfare-dependents.[21] However, examining the role of the state only allows for a partial understanding of citizenship and belonging, since individuals play a role in constituting themselves as a part of the state or nation. Magnifying the micro- and macro-level daily interactions of Haitian women illuminates the complex and dialectical processes through which they as individuals create the nation.

Everything from these daily, micro-level interactions to macro-level sociopolitical climates shapes migrants' relationship to the nation and influences their sense of belonging within the nation. Paid labor works at each of these levels to integrate, albeit conditionally, Haitian women into their new national contexts. At the macro level, the desire for migrants' labor, particularly in Boston and Montreal, at times facilitates migration and smooths migrants' entry to the paid workforce, as during Quebec's "Quiet Revolution" of the 1960s mentioned in chapter 1 and during a similar time period when employers in the United States sought out Haitians as low-wage domestic and factory workers. Though this route to migration allows certain migrants entry at certain times when it is convenient for the host nation, the employment options available often marginalize Haitian women based on their race and gender. At the micro level, Haitian women navigate workplace interactions and negotiate their relationships with coworkers and clients in ways that situate them as cultural citizens within their new national contexts.

The centrality of the capitalist economy to the contingencies of migration can naturalize, or denaturalize, foreigners as part of the nation due to their work ethic and behavior.[22] Devon Carbado separates the concepts of American citizenship and American identity, arguing that one can be a citizen but still excluded from the national identity.[23] Carbado's concept of "racial naturalization" shows how one can be excluded from citizenship by racial interpellation. I assert that cultural citizenship allows us to interrogate the ways in which foreigners negotiate national belonging, regardless of legal citizenship status. Cultural citizenship can also construct certain native-born people as "bad" citizens who are unworthy of an equal place in the nation. Ideals about work have played a crucial role in the construction of modern citizenship.[24] As citizenship, perhaps especially cultural citizenship, remains highly contingent on conduct, the expectation that model citizens will actively engage in the system of capitalism, both in action and in ideology, inextricably ties the concept of cultural citizenship to themes of paid labor and consumerism.

While some scholars identify economic and cultural citizenship as separate, in the experiences of Haitian women in diaspora, the two are in fact closely intertwined.[25] Given that the right to work and prosper is deeply entrenched in neoliberal cultural identity, work and employment are at the heart of cultural citizenship in neoliberal nation-states. For instance, through our interactions, Edwidge, in chapter 4, demonstrated that her role as a professional is central to her identity as a Haitian woman in the United States. She takes great pride in her work and was eager to invite me to her workplace so that I could see how valued and important she is in her job. As someone who has lived in the United States for decades, she has adopted the neoliberal ideals of hard work and self-sufficiency that are so ingrained in mainstream notions of what it means to be American. For Edwidge, as with many of the Haitian women in this study, economic citizenship and cultural citizenship are indistinguishable, as the economic and the cultural are so intertwined and these processes occur simultaneously. Including the centrality of paid labor in cultural citizenship allows us to look at economic citizenship and national belonging together as indivisible processes.

Social ties in the workplace are a tool through which processes of race, gender, and class take place, putting Haitian women into contact with others in their national context outside of the Haitian community. Coworkers, bosses, and clients interact with Haitian women in the workplace, establishing norms around how Haitian women relate to people of other races, ethnicities, classes, and genders, thereby situating Haitian women within their national contexts. In effect, these social ties act as a way to establish cultural citizenship through paid labor.

In the workplace, cultural citizenship plays an important role because racial groups and hierarchies are constructed and reconstructed through paid labor. People of different races and ethnicities come into contact in the workplace. Through this contact, immigrants and native-born people alike negotiate their positions within the workplace, and the nation, through their relationships to the paid workforce. Race becomes a crucial way in which Haitian women, and people in general, experience belonging within the national contexts in this study.

Similarly, gender and class intersect with cultural citizenship by situating Haitian women within the Haitian national context as well as their new cultural contexts. Migration offers an opportunity for a shift in gender roles. While sometimes that shift allows for a more even distribution of household labor between domestic partners, other times it leads to a re-entrenchment of old gender norms. Regardless, gender and class in Haiti shape experiences of gender and class in their new national contexts. Both in Haiti and abroad, gender and class, particularly as they intersect with paid labor, influence the lived experiences of national belonging.

I seek to highlight how the specific positioning of Haitian women within national and transnational matrices of power illuminates processes of inclusion and belonging within different national contexts. Employment serves as a mode of negotiating racism and obtaining a higher degree of cultural inclusion within the United States due to the American Dream ideology that ensures success through hard work and the myth of meritocracy. In this section I will provide a brief introduction to the term "cultural citizenship" to situate my usage of the term by examining how scholars discuss concepts that inform my understanding of cultural citizenship.[26]

Some scholars emphasize that citizenship is a legal category with enormous consequences. While I do not disagree with that assessment, my engagement with citizenship is in its cultural component. In Renato Rosaldo's example of cultural citizenship and educational change, he envisions the classroom dynamics within higher education shifting to include texts written by minorities alongside the classical texts of white men who have historically been in power.[27]

Unlike Rosaldo, I do not conceive of "cultural citizenship" as an oxymoronic phrase because I assert that culture is at the very heart of what it means to be a citizen; culture determines who is deemed an insider and who is deemed an outsider.

In this book I present the case of Haitian women living and working in diaspora and how their work circumstances play a central role in negotiating their belonging within the nation. Like the culture of the classroom described by Rosaldo, the culture of the workplace serves as a site where the culture of the nation is formed. Rosaldo suggests that a cultural shift in the curriculum can lead to a happy cultural pluralism where no set of cultural practices or forms is dominant in the classroom. I assert that dominant cultural formations always persist but that marginal cultural practices can slowly and minutely shift these dominant cultural formations through daily interactions. Those in power are not the only ones maintaining the national culture, but rather all members of the nation play a role in shaping senses of national belonging and cultural citizenship.

The manner in which I use the term "cultural citizenship" in this book closely resembles the way that Cati Coe describes what she calls political belonging. Coe states, "Political belonging is negotiated in everyday life."[28] Coe continues on to say, "Work gives people social identity and status, both within the workplace and the wider political community."[29] The themes in this book in terms of work as a source of social identity deeply resonate with Coe's findings; however, the purpose of this book is not to look exclusively at inclusion within a political community but rather at belonging within the nation more broadly. Though Coe makes a strong argument regarding her use of the term "political belonging," I maintain that it is not particularly helpful or necessary to conflate a general sense of belonging with political citizenship. Coe stretches the term "political" to include belonging in a way that extends beyond common understanding of what "political" typically entails. Coe defines a political unit as everything from the nation-state to ethnic groups and even humanity.[30] I argue that while not all belonging is necessarily political in all cases, belonging is absolutely cultural in nature.

Cultural citizenship is about a sense of belonging that does not necessarily map onto legal belonging or having a voice in the affairs of state and politics. Cultural citizenship is about the cognitive boundaries of the nation. It is about determining who belongs. By default, the other side of belonging involves determining who does not belong. Rather than an inclusion of difference in a pluralistic manner as Rosaldo imagines it, I see cultural citizenship as comprised of degrees of belonging within the dominant national culture. Culture consists of practices and symbols that communicate meaning. National culture can be expressed through dress, demeanor, language, food, and social networks. Though nations typically have multiple cultural expressions, there are usually dominant cultural forms and practices that are widely recognized as representative of the nation. For instance, the French language is a cultural practice of France as a nation, even though not every individual within the nation may speak French. Culture is realized through social networks in that it is shared through relationships.

Scholar Alyshia Gálvez is concerned that the concept of cultural citizenship can reify the state's power by suggesting that the state has had a clear plan with regard to crafting legal citizenship.[31] I view citizenship as a large and multifaceted concept, of which the legal component is one part of the greater whole that is inextricably linked with social, economic, and cultural citizenship. When analyzing cultural citizenship, this book examines the social and economic components of cultural citizenship. I use the term "cultural citizenship" because I am analyzing citizenship through the lens of culture, and I focus on the extra-juridical components of it.

Contrary to Gálvez's study of citizenship among undocumented Mexican immigrants in the United States, many of the women in this study migrated via mostly legal avenues and secured legal citizenship in their host nations.[32] In Gálvez's study, mobility was an important concern for the undocumented migrants because their legal citizenship status seriously limited their ability to cross the U.S.-Mexico border. The socioeconomic class of the Haitian migrants in this study enabled them to migrate with visas and green cards and to travel back and forth between Haiti and their new homes in Boston, Montreal, and Paris.

In examining the uneven incorporation of Puerto Ricans into U.S. society, Juan Flores challenges the idea of assimilation. Flores writes, "Rather than being subsumed and repressed, Puerto Rican culture contributes, on its own terms and as an extension of its own traditions, to a new amalgam of human expression. It is the existing racial, national and class divisions in U.S. society which allow for, indeed necessitate, this alternative course of cultural change."[33] For Flores, it does not make sense to think of Puerto Rican culture in terms of assimilation in any traditional sense. Instead, he views Puerto Rican culture as contributing to U.S. society in complex ways, including engagement with Black American cultural forms in New York. Similarly, this study examines Haitian participation in the national cultures of their new homes in dynamic ways that challenge traditional assumptions about the process of assimilation or stripping away one's prior identity to adopt a new national culture.

Following from Flores, Adelaida Del Castillo discusses social citizenship with regard to undocumented Mexican immigrants in the United States in ways that are both similar and dissimilar to my conceptualization of cultural citizenship.[34] Like cultural citizenship, the concept of social citizenship that Del Castillo deploys argues that for these undocumented immigrants, social citizenship is not dependent on legal or political citizenship. Del Castillo defines social citizenship as working and paying taxes to fulfill the social duties of citizenship.[35] Though cultural citizenship does involve one's relationship to the paid workforce, it more concerns the cultural practices that organize daily lives rather than the paying of taxes and using social services. In this way, cultural citizenship is less quantifiable in that it describes the affective and experiential dimensions of social and cultural belonging.

In a related theoretical framework, scholar Orly Clerge studies Black migrants, including Haitians, in the United States, presenting the concept of racial capitalism. She explains the concept as, "Racism and nationalism are key factors in the economic system of exchange and production."[36] Clerge ties racial capitalism to the global political economy, stating, "The term *racial capitalism* provides a lens to analyze how the global economy is built on the assignment of value and power to workers based on the racial categories they are put into."[37] My further development of the concept of cultural citizenship intersects with Clerge's concept of racial capitalism in that my definition of cultural citizenship centers around the position of workers and how that position ties them to the nation and the global political economy.

Some scholars suggest that citizenship may no longer be an appropriate way to understand our increasingly transnational world; however, I argue that nations continue to hold great significance in this era of transnationalism, and so long as nations persist, the belonging within nations, also known as citizenship, is still pertinent to the lives of people around the world. Thus, cultural citizenship is neither completely independent of nor directly reducible to legal citizenship. It is a framework for negotiating differential levels of inclusion and exclusion through the lens of work, race, gender, and social ties to understand cultural belonging within the nation.

Feminist theories of race and paid labor provide a basis for understanding the intersecting power relations at play for Haitian women within the global political economy. Following the work of Marxist feminist scholars, I argue that paid labor is inseparable from issues of gender, culture, and the global political economy.[38] Early Marxist feminists argued that women's oppression is rooted in their relationship to the means of production vis-à-vis men.[39] Some have suggested that women's employment outside the home is empowering and leads to greater gender equality in the household. This argument largely evolved from studies of white, middle-class, heterosexual women in the United States as they have struggled to gain gender equality within the workforce.

Gender and Migration

This section outlines the scholarly literature linking migration to analyses of gender and transnationalism to emphasize the importance of gender and migration to the study of cultural citizenship. First, literature on gender and migration helps to situate my analysis of the shifting relationship between Haitian women and both paid and unpaid domestic labor upon migration, which I argue is an important site where cultural citizenship is negotiated.

Since gender inevitably shapes migrants' ability to relocate and find employment, migration must be considered through a gendered lens to understand fully the processes at play.[40] The feminization of migration and the political economy of the receiving nations combine to establish gendered migration patterns of women from Haiti. Keeping gender in focus is particularly important when looking at the Haitian diaspora, as women have frequently been the first to move to North America and France with other family members following later. In the past several decades, West Indian women, rather than men, have dominated migration from the Caribbean to the United States, with women often moving before the rest of their families.[41] This is at least in part due to the fact that it has been much easier for women from the Caribbean to obtain U.S. work visas.[42] Migration studies have developed over time to include more of a focus on women, in recent decades turning toward a focus on intersectional approaches that critically examine the confluence of gender, class, and race.[43] A careful analysis of the experiences of women requires an intersectional approach to unpack the many social, racial, and economic forces that shape their experiences locally and transnationally.

Some scholars view the specific focus on women and migration to be a stage in the evolution of migration studies but contend that we need to move past "gender segregation" in migration studies in sociology.[44] Scholars have argued that gender and migration studies have "moved from the recovery of women's experiences, to the mainstreaming of gender within migration studies, to intersectionality."[45] I argue that the work of "recovering" women's experiences, particularly of women of color, is far from complete and that adding the experiences of women to the discourse and using intersectional analysis are in no way mutually exclusive. In fact, a focus specifically on the experiences of women requires an intersectional approach to unpack the many social, racial, and economic forces that shape their experiences of cultural citizenship. The feminization of migration framework overshadows intersectional experiences of women. While we should certainly not rely on a segregated approach to studying gender and migration that reinforces problematic categories, neither should we abandon analyses that specifically focus on the experiences of women for fear of having those studies marginalized in mainstream sociological discourse on migration.

Migration studies has developed over time to include more of a focus on women, but many scholars turned toward a focus on gender without using an intersectional approach that critically examines the confluence of gender, class, and race.[46] Scholars using an intersectional approach in migration studies are beginning to fill the gap in the literature.[47] Through this study I add to the work of scholars who are critically engaging with gender as it intersects with race and migration.

By focusing on the experiences of Haitian women in my research, I do not intend to analyze women as an essential monolithic category. That being said, I do think that gender role prescriptions in Haiti and structures of gender oppression in the West influence the ways in which Haitian women experience migration and belonging within the nation. My focus specifically on Haitian women aims to fill a gap in research literature where the experiences of Haitian women have not been brought to the forefront, as most studies of Haitian immigrants to date have heavily focused on the experiences of Haitian men, with some notable exceptions.[48] Simultaneously, I seek to demonstrate the ways in which the experiences of Haitian women reveal important facets of processes of inclusion and belonging in the nation, with implications for other migrant groups and native-born citizens.

In illuminating how Haitian women's experiences show us realities of inclusion and belonging, I also draw attention to the different levels at which Haitian women function individually, locally, nationally, and transnationally. Patricia Pessar and Sarah Mahler discuss gendered geographies of power, arguing, "Gender operates simultaneously on multiple spatial and social scales (e.g., the body, the family, the state) across transnational terrains."[49] According to Pessar and Mahler, the "'gendered geographies of power' is a framework for analyzing people's gendered social agency—corporal and cognitive—given their own initiative as well as their positioning within multiple hierarchies of power operative within and across many terrains."[50] When read alongside cultural citizenship, Pessar and Mahler's concept of gendered geographies of power plays into the ways that Haitian women are active agents in negotiating their positioning within the nation in response to various oppressive forces that shape their daily experiences. Next, the literature on transnational migrant ties provides a context to more fully understand the complicated webs of affective, economic, and political belonging that shape the lives of Haitian women in diaspora. While many Haitian migrants fully incorporate into the workforce and some gain both cultural and legal citizenship, they often maintain transnational ties as well. Scholars of migration studies and Haitian studies have begun to shift the focus from traditional migration theory grounded in binary oppositions between countries of origin and countries of arrival to transnational theories of migration in which migrants participate in multiple national contexts simultaneously.

Transnational Ties

In addition to a shift toward intersectional research, many scholars of migration have moved from a traditional model of sending country versus host country to a transnational model that encompasses the complexities of migrants' experiences with regard to national ties.[51] Some scholars unpack the various types of transnational social spaces and transnational social practices that exist with regard to international migration. Thomas Faist, for example, examines transnational ties in terms of transnational parenting and family.[52] These transnational ties illustrate how cultural citizenship in a new host society can exist simultaneously with cultural citizenship in a migrant's country of origin; the two are not mutually exclusive but are instead deeply intertwined.

Transnational ties may serve a number of purposes for Haitian migrants, including ways to navigate issues of oppression and discrimination in their new homes. Maintaining transnational ties to Haiti may offer a support system of other Haitians in diaspora; Haitian identity unifies many in Boston, Montreal, and Paris, enabling the formation of diasporic groups to maintain Haitian culture, stay informed about Haitian politics, and send remittances or aid to Haiti. Strong transnational ties, both cultural and economic, strengthen and unite Haitians across the globe. Transnational ties facilitate migration for Haitians, as many join family members or existing Haitian communities when they move to the United States, Canada, and France. Upon arrival, many Haitian migrants find housing and employment through networks in the Haitian community in their new homes. These supportive systems of sharing survival strategies remain rooted in the strength of a shared Haitian identity.

These transnational ties may also influence the way that Haitian migrants conceptualize themselves and their role in society as they develop survival strategies. Conceptualizing one's position in North America and Europe as temporary rather than permanent may help immigrants to cope with some of the oppression that they face on a daily basis.[53] By keeping their social and economic positions in Haiti in mind, immigrants may reject full incorporation into their new societies on some level. In this way, they take control of their degree of cultural citizenship through daily interactions and attitudes that intentionally keep themselves separate from fully belonging within the nation.

Various scholars call attention to the ways in which migrants maintain transnational ties, looking at citizenship in light of migration. Irene Bloemraad et al. posit that "globalization challenges simple understandings of citizenship as state-centered and state-controlled" but maintain that nation-states continue to wield a great deal of power over citizenship in terms of rights and belonging.[54] Bloemraad et al. explore literature that clearly situates citizenship within national borders as well as scholarship that calls national borders into question. They suggest that future research should highlight immigrants' agency in defining and negotiating citizenship, providing an opportunity to center transnational ties that immigrants continue to nurture post-migration. This current study on cultural citizenship follows from Bloemraad et al.'s call for research examining immigrants' active role in negotiating their belonging within the nation.

Scholars of Haitian studies have used a transnational lens to analyze Haitian diasporic relationships for decades.[55] In particular, *Nations Unbound* by Linda Basch et al. offers an analysis of transnational processes that shape Haiti as a nation, including organizations in diaspora that enable Haitians abroad to stay connected to Haitian national identity, politics, and economic structure through remittances.[56]

Georges Woke Up Laughing, a monograph about Georges Fouron, a Haitian scholar who migrated to New York and one of the authors, remains an important work within Haitian diasporic literature that highlights the complex transnational ties that immigrants maintain.[57] The authors define "transmigrants" as immigrants who "live their lives across borders. . . . Transmigrants live within a transnational social field that extends into countries around the world in which family members or compatriots have settled. They live in two or more nation-states."[58] The monograph illustrates the concept of "transmigrant" and demonstrates how the population of Haiti stretches across the bounds of the nation-state. I borrow the term "transmigrant" to describe the Haitian women in this study, drawing on the theorization by Schiller and Fouron that justifies the use of the term to describe the transnational component of immigrants' lives.

Also examining transnational ties and Haiti, Manuel Orozco and Elisabeth Burgess examine the practice of sending remittances particularly in light of the 2010 earthquake in Haiti, ultimately coming to the conclusion that the Haitian diaspora can only contribute within their means and that more of an emphasis should be placed on ensuring that members of the diaspora in the United States develop and thrive as part of Haiti's reconstruction plan.[59] Orozco and Burgess's analysis looks at Haitians in diaspora in terms of both their place within the Haitian national economy and their place within the United States' economy. Though using other terms, Orozco and Burgess's study of remittances links Haitian reconstruction levels with levels of cultural and economic citizenship.

Methods

Following from the works of Rhacel Salazar Parreñas and Ernesto Castañeda, this multisited ethnography makes connections between the larger context of the global political economy and the lived experiences of Haitian women in diaspora.[60] Though often confused with comparative methods, a multisited ethnography moves "beyond a superficial comparison between groups, instead tracing threads across space to investigate a subject of inquiry that is not confined to a single site."[61] As I wrote in a past article, "According to [George]

Marcus, 'different related sites can be designated differently for ethnographic treatment.' In other words, not every site requires the same level of thick description. For some sites, perhaps a thin description will suffice in making the broader analysis. The researcher needs to be very self-reflexive about the production of field sites and the level of interrogation (thick/thin) necessary in each site."[62]

Overall, this project consists of ethnographic fieldwork and semistructured interviews with Haitian women in the Boston, Montreal, and Paris metropolitan areas from 2011 to 2017, with a combination of extended stays and shorter visits to each of the three cities during this time. I began the initial stages of data collection for this project in 2011 with ethnographic fieldwork and in-depth interviews with Haitian women in Boston. As one of the largest sites of the Haitian diaspora in the United States, yet seriously understudied compared with New York and Miami, it made sense as an interesting field site where I could expand on existing literature about the Haitian diaspora, such as *Mama Lola: A Vodou Priestess in Brooklyn*, *Georges Woke Up Laughing: Long-distance Nationalism and the Search for Home*, and *The New Noir: Race, Identity, and Diaspora in Black Suburbia*.[63] For instance, in *Mama Lola*, Karen McCarthy Brown provides an ethnographic work following Mama Lola's life in New York.[64] This book supplements the ethnographic narrative provided by McCarthy Brown by centering the lives of middle- and upper-class Haitian women, none of whom so much as mentioned Vodou in our interviews, presumably because of the class implications associated with Vodou; Vodou is considered a religion of the common Haitian person, whereas affluent Haitians tend to cling to Christianity, at least publicly.

As stated at the start of this introduction, my mother never taught my brother and me so much as a word of Kreyòl. My Haitian mother, a baptized Roman Catholic who still regularly attends church, supposedly does not believe in Vodou, though she is very superstitious and afraid of it.[65] I was an adult before I learned that my grandmother, a dark-skinned Haitian woman who passed when I was twelve, was a practitioner of Vodou. My mother never spoke of Vodou and claimed to have very limited knowledge of it. She built a life for herself in the United States, emphasizing parts of her culture that were respected and rewarded and suppressing the parts of her Haitian identity that were stigmatized and feared. Paired with *Mama Lola*, this book illustrates the great diversity that exists within Haitian society, and more specifically, within the Haitian diaspora.

This study focuses on a small sample size in specific geographic locations; therefore, the results will not broadly represent the experiences of all, or even most, Haitian immigrants. However, focusing on a small sample proves useful in going beyond the limitations of existing conceptual frameworks by allowing me to establish strong relationships with many of the participants that have endured long past the end of my fieldwork. Though the interviews in this study are in no way representative of the experiences of all Haitian immigrants, I argue that aspects of their experiences point to larger processes of belonging and inclusion.

I recruited participants for this project through use of a "snowball sampling" method, beginning with participants in my social and professional networks and asking initial participants for referrals to other women who might be willing to participate in the study. All but one of the participants were born in Haiti and spent their early childhoods there prior to emigrating. The remaining participant was born in Florida to Haitian parents and immediately moved back to Haiti to spend her early childhood.

Outline of Chapters

The following chapters engage with race, gender, and cultural citizenship through multisited ethnography. Some chapters of this book focus more heavily on one of the sites than the others, but each chapter includes at least one experience or perspective from each site. Unlike in a comparative study where one might devote a chapter to each site or present data from each site equally throughout, this study shifts back and forth between sites to articulate themes as they arise. For instance, chapter 4 on gender and class focuses primarily on the experiences of Haitian women in Boston, as that is where the themes of gender and class were articulated most clearly. That is not to say that the theme was only present in Boston, but that something about the Boston context drew out those themes in a way that could shed light on present but otherwise difficult-to-see patterns in the other two sites. Chapter 2, however, focuses primarily on data from Montreal to elucidate the ways that social ties in the workplace situate Haitian women within their new national contexts while pulling in a few examples from Boston and Paris as well. This approach to organizing the analysis reflects the fluidity of the Haitian diaspora and the way that themes of race, gender, and national belonging exist across the diaspora while acknowledging that these themes are more readily visible in certain places at certain times.

Chapter 1 provides a brief overview of the sociopolitical contexts of the three sites, offering some context to the environments that Haitian women faced upon arrival in their new homes. Each of the sites possesses a unique history and sociopolitical context, shaping the experiences of Haitian women in distinct, yet connected, ways.

Chapter 2 examines the role of social ties in the workplace and how those social ties situate Haitian women within the nation in inclusionary, exclusionary, or contradictory ways.

In chapter 3, I employ a transnational approach to uncover the historical contexts that shape understandings of race and ethnicity as modalities in which social membership and cultural citizenship are experienced and to illuminate the ways in which national ideology combined with relationships to the paid workforce function as a powerful influence in the daily lives of Haitian women.

Chapters 4 and 5 look at issues of class and gender more explicitly than other chapters in this book, shedding light on the ways in which Haitian women of the first wave of migration frequently experienced a shift in class position and gender roles upon migration.

Building on chapters 2 through 5, chapter 6 examines the ways in which daily workplace interactions constitute acts of creating cultural citizenship. Haitian women establish the cognitive contours of the nation through those daily interactions that are connected to their paid labor outside the home. Chapter 6 ties theories of cultural citizenship to the daily lived experiences of Haitian women, illustrating the ways in which Haitian women shape the nation from the ground up while simultaneously being influenced by politics and macro structures of power. Finally, the conclusion reflects on events in Haiti and the lives of my participants since the end of the fieldwork and contemplates areas for future research.

1

Haiti in a Global Context

Haiti has long been at the center of the transnational circuits that created the foundation for emigration to the present day. Haiti's colonial history dates back to 1492 when Columbus landed on the shores of the island of Hispaniola (modern-day Haiti and the Dominican Republic) during his first voyage to the New World. Although Hispaniola was initially colonized by the Spanish, the French established their first major settlement on the western part of the island in 1670. Spain surrendered sovereignty of the western part of the island, referred to as Saint-Domingue, to France in 1697. Saint-Domingue came to play a central role in France's economy through its particularly cruel and abusive slave labor system. In response to the harsh conditions in Saint-Domingue, African slaves and mulattoes in the colony rallied together to stage a massive slave revolt against the French. August 14, 1791, marked the beginning of the Haitian Revolution, a slave revolt that defeated Napoleon's army and led to Haitian independence in January of 1804.[1]

Following the revolution, Haiti spent over fifty years fighting a battle of international diplomacy to gain recognition as an independent nation-state while the international community, notably the United States, France, and the Vatican, refused to come to terms with the implications of an independent Black nation.[2] France demanded that Haiti pay reparations to compensate for the economic loss of the colony, since France had been extracting incredible amounts of wealth from the exploitation of slaves and their labor. Being forced to pay reparations after winning independence put a huge economic strain on the new nation, setting the stage for serious political instability, including a military occupation by the United States beginning in 1915 that lasted for a period of nineteen years.

The largely unwelcome U.S. military presence suppressed democracy in Haiti with claims that Haitians were inferior and incapable of governing themselves.[3] The period of U.S. occupation was marked by blatant racism, violence, and the manipulation of Haitian resources to benefit American interests.

The occupation officially ended in 1934 when the United States finally withdrew troops but continued to play a large role in Haiti both politically and financially.[4] A few decades after the end of U.S. occupation marked the start of the brutally repressive Duvalier dictatorship. The hereditary dictatorship, first led by Francois "Papa Doc" Duvalier, then by his son, Jean-Claude "Baby Doc" Duvalier, lasted almost thirty years, from 1957 to 1986.[5] Foreign governments continued to play a large role in Haitian politics following the Duvalier dictatorship by supporting political candidates who aligned with foreign interests and by orchestrating the coup d'état that overthrew President Jean-Bertrand Aristide in 1991. Most recently, prominent interventions in Haiti have taken the form of foreign aid with restrictive conditions and the proliferation of activity by nongovernmental organizations, which some scholars suggest has become a form of neocolonialism.[6]

While Haitians have migrated to other sites in the Caribbean for many years, such as the flow of immigrant workers from Haiti to Cuba and the Dominican Republic during the United States' occupation of Haiti in the early twentieth century, the first major flow of Haitian emigration outside the Caribbean occurred during the Duvalier regime.[7] Under the dictatorship, many intellectuals and members of the political opposition fled to the United States, Canada, and France, since these governments had historically played a large role in Haitian politics.[8]

Although many migrants sought refuge from the dictatorship in Canada and the United States, both countries supported the violent and oppressive Duvalier regime that triggered the first major wave of immigration; the United States in an effort to defend against communism in the Caribbean, and Canada in an economic sense as, though Canada had never occupied Haiti officially as the United States had, several Canadian banks had opened in Haiti during the Duvalier dictatorship in order to advance Canadian business interests. Canada's financial investments there then continued to fuel the out-migration of Haitians, many of whom landed in Montreal, while the United States was reticent when it came to offering asylum to political refugees under the Duvalier regime.[9]

The first wave of immigrants consisted almost exclusively of middle- and upper-class Haitians, many of whom encountered poverty and discrimination as a result of migrating. In order to make a living, Haitian immigrants had to enter the workforce in subordinate roles, many taking jobs in service industries, especially in health care as medical office staff, aides, and hospital workers.[10] Although these migrants sought the United States, Canada, and France as temporary refuges rather than long-term homes, many remained in these nations permanently.

In 1991, President Jean-Bertrand Aristide used his political position to encourage a transnational conceptualization of Haiti by declaring the Haitian diaspora the "10th Department" of the Haitian state. Though legally the state did not permit dual citizenship, by declaring the diaspora an official department of Haiti, Aristide made a strong statement regarding the integral role that the diaspora plays in Haiti culturally, politically, and economically.[11] Haitian Americans, for example, maintain relationships with Haiti but also with diasporic communities in Montreal, Paris, and Santo Domingo in the Dominican Republic.[12] Additionally, the Haitian political landscape is deeply transnational, with key players living in Montreal, Paris, New York, and other sites in the Haitian diaspora.[13] Many Haitians have also migrated throughout the Caribbean, including locations such as Cuba, since early on in Haitian history.

This study focuses on three metropolitan areas, one in each country, the United States, Canada, and France, in which many Haitians have made their homes and developed thriving diasporic communities: Boston, Montreal, and Paris. The following sections provide a brief snapshot of the history of each city's relationship to Haiti and Haitian migrants in each case study.

National Sociopolitical Contexts

The national approach to immigration and to integration of cultural difference in each of the field sites influences Haitian women's ability to migrate and how they are able to forge cultural citizenship for themselves. Each nation's historical relationship to immigration shapes the contemporary climate that immigrants experience when attempting to become a part of the nation. France's colonial past and associated tensions with regard to understanding its relationship to former colonies certainly influences France's approach to immigration and cultural integration. The United States' history of forced migration from Africa and chattel slavery remains a specter as the United States struggles to come to terms with its past and present relationship to people of the African diaspora, both native-born Americans and immigrants. Though slavery was legal in Canada for a time, it did not experience slavery to the same extent that France and the United States did, though Quebec certainly benefited from slavery as a French colony. For Quebec, its history as a former colony of France, and a desire to maintain that relationship to France as part of Quebec's national identity, makes Quebec a minority nation that is fighting to protect its identity within the larger nation of Canada. Canada has adopted an assimilationist approach to Quebec, aiming to diminish the province's unique linguistic profile and to unify Canada as an anglophone nation.

Canada and the United States have both adopted multicultural approaches to national identity. Multicultural political projects manifest themselves differently in each nation, yet the rhetoric of multiculturalism always suggests that the nation-state recognizes and values the cultural diversity of its citizens. This ideal of embracing a multiplicity of cultures within the nation, however, often comes into conflict with the lived realities of people within a nominally "multicultural" nation where policies and dominant cultural norms can stand in tension with the goal of respecting cultural diversity.[14] For example, while the national ideology of the United States has evolved over time, from assimilationism to cultural pluralism (and in the 1990s to a multicultural approach), heated debates persist regarding bilingual education in schools, rights of immigrants, religious pluralism, and anxieties over growing minority populations.[15]

France, on the other hand, has taken a universalist approach, which in theory erases all differences in an attempt to make every French citizen "the same." The nation goes so far as to prohibit the collection of information regarding race and ethnicity in the national census.

The United States of America

In the United States during the 1960s and 1970s, it was much easier for Haitian women than men to gain work visas, as many employers sought Haitian women as cheap domestic laborers due to their reputation for having a strong work ethic and their willingness to work for low wages. Haitian women remain the driving force behind the Haitian community in Boston. Perhaps resulting from the particular migration pattern in which women were frequently the first in their families to migrate to Boston, Haitian diasporic networks there continue to center around women's social ties. Unlike in Montreal, where the community center Maison d'Haïti provides a clear focal point for the Haitian community, in Boston, informal familial and social networks are the primary sites where Haitian culture is maintained. Haitian women organize many of the informal gatherings of Haitians that take place in the home and play a crucial role in sustaining smaller organizations serving the Haitian community in Boston. Similar to how the diasporic community functions in Montreal, these informal familial and social networks in Boston play an important role in helping many Haitian migrants find their first employment after moving to the Boston area. Immigration patterns from Haiti to the United States in the first wave of migration involved Haitian women immigrating as the first in their family, a pattern consistent with migration flows of the Global South. The types of jobs available to new migrant women typically entail underpaid and insecure forms of caring labor.

Boston, Massachusetts. Massachusetts is home to the third largest Haitian community in the United States, following Florida and New York. The Haitian community in Massachusetts has played an important role in the cultural and economic life of the state for upwards of fifty years. As of 2019, there were an estimated 68,800 people of Haitian ancestry in the Boston metropolitan area.[16]

Twenty percent of Haitians in Boston work in health care support occupations, including as registered nurses and in administrative support positions.[17]

Beginning with the first wave of Haitian migrants in the late 1950s, the number of people of Haitian ancestry in the United States continues to grow steadily, with an estimated 290,000 people in 1990, 548,000 in 2000, 830,000 in 2009, and approximately 1.1 million in 2021.[18] Immigration to Boston expanded significantly in the 1960s, particularly following the 1965 Immigration Act; however, by the 1990s and onward many policies, at both the national and local levels, have made immigration to Boston more challenging. Haitian elite began to arrive in Boston in the 1960s and 1970s, fleeing the Duvalier regime and paving the way for middle- and working-class Haitians to immigrate in the 1970s and 1980s. Many Haitians first migrated to New York and then continued to Boston within anytime from days to years to reunite with family.

Haitians in the first wave of migration to Boston in the 1960s and 1970s found themselves suddenly embroiled in violent race riots over the desegregation of schools. In 1965, the state designated forty-five schools as being racially imbalanced and implemented the process of busing students to schools outside their neighborhoods to address educational segregation. This attempt at desegregating schools touched off violent protests and enflamed racial tensions in the city.[19] Caught in the middle of long-standing racial tensions between white and African American residents of the city, Haitian migrants shared the brunt of the anger that many white residents directed at all Black people. As in other U.S. destinations for Haitian migrants, Boston's long history of racial tensions seriously influenced the inclusion and exclusion of Haitians.

According to Marilynn S. Johnson, author of *The New Bostonians*, poorer and less educated Haitians followed suit and immigrated to Boston in the 1990s to flee political and economic instability.[20] While many Haitians in the first wave of immigration to Boston were able to come through family unification processes, many of the subsequent waves from the 1980s onward arrived as unauthorized migrants. Some of those unauthorized migrants, particularly in the wake of the devastating 2010 earthquake, were granted asylum or temporary visas.[21]

Nonetheless, these "newer migrants have been crucial in re-building the population, labor force, and metropolitan landscape of the new Boston."[22] Boston's economy went through a period of restructuring and economic growth around the turn of the millennium in which immigrant workers made up the vast majority of the city's new workforce, with the city relying heavily on immigrant labor to support its growing service-based economy.[23]

Quebec, Canada

Since the mid-twentieth century, Quebec has sought out highly skilled immigrants to replace its aging population, taking control of immigration from the Canadian national government. Immigration patterns to Quebec were very similar to immigration patterns to Canada as a whole until 1991, when Quebec gained control of immigration for the province.[24]

Quebec reinforced its unique national identity as a francophone nation within Canada through immigration while simultaneously increasing diversity by welcoming immigrants from a range of French-speaking countries around the world. Cory Blad and Philippe Couton write, "Quebec's understanding of immigration has changed radically and it is now becoming a bona fide immigrant society after two centuries of relative isolation, periods of mass emigration and a general suspicion of immigration."[25]

Though Canada is commonly understood to be a multicultural nation, scholars frequently describe Quebec as an "intercultural nation" in which immigrants "are encouraged to retain their traditional beliefs and values; however the pre-existing dominant public milieu is institutionally protected."[26] According to some scholars, "Quebec's policy of interculturalism can be characterized as a 'hybrid' between Canadian multiculturalism and French republicanism."[27] While the diversity of immigrants has changed the demographic makeup of Quebec, this diversity is centered around the national norm of the French language.[28]

Quebec nationalists feared losing Quebec's distinctly francophone cultural identity, so as more immigrants moved to Quebec, the focus became "convergence" around the French language as the key to welcoming foreigners without losing Quebec's francophone cultural identity.[29] According to Blad and Couton, "not only is immigration not challenging traditional nation-statehood, it is reinforcing it."[30] Highly skilled francophone immigrants experience higher levels of unemployment and deskilling as well as lower income when compared with native-born Quebecers and previous cohorts of immigrants. This is in large part due to employers not recognizing foreign diplomas and experiences, immigrants not having access to the same local social networks that provide job opportunities, and discrimination.[31] Stereotypes of women immigrants include the idea that Black women are too slow to work as nurses and that Maghrebi women are oppressed by their cultures if they wear a hijab. A surge in Islamophobia following the 9/11 terrorist attack in the United States made it particularly difficult for migrant women from the Maghreb to integrate.[32]

Haitian migration to Quebec clearly illustrates how conditional inclusion of migrants based on their labor creates tensions as inclusion chafes against the power of the elite. Prior to 1962, Canada legally used race as a criterion by which to evaluate potential migrants.[33] The need for an increased labor force led Canada to change this policy, with the change being fully implemented in 1967. While traditionally immigrants to Canada came from Europe, this shift in policy led to major immigration increases from the Global South.[34] Following the economic, cultural, and political Quiet Revolution of the 1960s, Quebec had a serious shortage of skilled laborers. Breaking with a tradition of excluding foreigners in favor of preserving Quebec's ethnic identity, the province of Quebec then actively sought out trained middle- and upper-class professionals to fill its workforce. Since Quebec viewed its national identity as a distinct ethnic and linguistic group under siege, recruitment of non-Quebecois francophone workers was therefore a necessary, but fraught, decision. Haiti and Quebec's shared history with French colonialism made highly educated Haitians a more attractive group than potential anglophone immigrants, as the necessity of maintaining Quebec's French roots was paramount in the maintenance of Quebec's national identity; yet Haitian immigrants' Blackness is still noted and often becomes a source of rejection. As Quebec and Canada engaged with issues of diversity and multiculturalism, according to Blad and Couton, "The issue that soon faced the Quebec state was, however, not an attack on its national sovereignty by the federal government. Rather the larger challenge was the increasing ethno-cultural diversity in Quebec as a result of global market integration."[35] Canada-Quebec immigration agreements from 1971 to 1991 gave Quebec increased provincial rights regarding immigration, though the Quebec government continues to press for additional powers when it comes to immigration.[36]

Montreal. The first major wave of Haitian migrants arrived in the French-speaking Canadian province of Quebec. Located on the eastern side of Canada, Quebec is the only French-speaking province within an otherwise anglophone nation. This migration occurred during the period known in Quebec as *la révolution tranquille*—the quiet revolution—toward an increasingly secular state which allowed for the migration of primarily upper-class, French-speaking Haitians to take professional jobs in the province.[37] This first wave of migrants was temporarily accepted into the nation because of their professional and French language skills. Quebec began recruiting Haitians only after first attempting to recruit French-speaking Europeans, as Quebec deemed white, French-speaking Europeans as more easily a part of their national identity than Black Haitians.

By 1974, Haitian migrants made up the largest number of migrants coming to Quebec, accounting for 14.5 percent of total incoming migrants.[38] When increasing numbers of lower-class Haitians began to migrate to Quebec in subsequent years, the provincial and national governments determined that highly skilled laborers were more welcome to join the nation than French-speaking working-class Haitians, shifting to an immigration policy that prioritized labor-ability over race and ethnicity, thus doubling the class impediments to migration for poor and working-class migrants.

The pattern of shifting tactics for recruiting and controlling migrants indicates several priorities when determining who could be a part of Quebec's population. Quebec acted in ways that made clear that white, French-speaking, highly skilled laborers were the most attractive immigrants. This history reveals the interconnectedness of race, labor, and class in who was included in the nation. Today, Haitians are one of the largest non-European ethnic groups in Canada. As of 2016, approximately 80,000 Haitians lived in Montreal.[39] The diversity of the Haitian population in Montreal is reflective of the diversity within Haitian society and also reflective of the varied paths to integration experienced by differing waves of migrants.[40]

Today, Montreal is a bustling urban hub that is home to many racial, ethnic, and religious groups, including a vibrant Haitian community. Despite the diversity that fuels the region culturally and economically, in 2017 the government produced a film about the city that only depicted white French Canadians for the 375-year celebration of Montreal's founding. Citizens of Montreal raised an uproar over the blatant erasure of the province's diverse population, and the government quickly retracted the video. Each time I spoke with any Haitian woman the week of the video's release, with a dismayed shake of the head she would cite this video as a blatant example of Quebec's lingering race problems. This seemingly small instance represented larger tensions around the conditional inclusion of migrants in Quebec and indicated that there is much work to be done in terms of challenging dominant ideologies about Quebec's ethnic identity. The Haitian women with whom I spoke that week were frustrated, but they were also committed to raising awareness and working as citizens of Quebec to shape the nation. Their Haitian identities served as a principal unifying force that enabled them to organize, network, and resist the whitewashing of Montreal.

Due to the circumstances under which "highly skilled" middle- and upperclass Haitians first migrated to Quebec in numbers, Montreal is now home to thriving Haitian communities with strong, long-lasting institutions. In 2016, Montreal's Maison d'Haïti celebrated the opening of a beautiful new facility that is home to countless programs, social services, community archives, and cultural events. A core group of Haitian intellectuals established the Haitian community in Montreal over forty years ago, paving the way for later immigrants to continue to build and strengthen the community over time. The strong Haitian community in Montreal, which emerged within these particular sociopolitical circumstances, supports the cultural integration of many Haitian women by aiding with job placements both formally and through informal networking. The racism faced by early migrants in Montreal, though certainly present, was arguably less overt and violent than the racism that greeted Haitians in Boston during an era marked by antibusing riots and desegregation.

France

France's universalist approach to its cultural identity follows from the French Republican ideology that emerged during the French Revolution. Even today, hundreds of years after the Revolution, French national belonging still rests on disavowing any signs of a person's life prior to becoming part of the secular and indivisible French nation. However, this universalist ideal breaks down in the face of markers of identity, such as skin color and religion, which immigrants cannot or do not shed upon joining the French nation. Claims of universality notwithstanding, the underlying assumption is that the universal French (wo) man is white and Christian or secular. Most visibly, we see the breakdown of French universalism in controversies surrounding the bans on wearing religious headscarves in French public schools in 2004 and the abaya in 2023.[41] These bans against markers of Islam speak to the large Muslim population in France, in part from Algeria, a former French colony that won its independence from France in a revolutionary war in 1962. Though headscarves are seen as a sign of difference, crucifixes fit within the framework of "normal" Frenchness, high-lighting the hypocrisy of France's supposedly secular national identity. Even as recently as August 2023, the French minister of education announced a ban on the wearing of the abaya in public schools, which takes the discourse about the headscarf a step further by relying entirely on perceived differences in the wearer for what counts as an abaya as opposed to a dress.[42]

As this new controversy about the abaya illustrates, issues of immigration and integration continue to take center stage in French politics. France has used the term "integration" as key to securing a pluralist liberal democracy. This concept stems back to American functionalism in which "society's need for an order that overcomes conflict and differences pulls a harmonious, socially inclusive unity based on 'value integration.'"[43] The Chicago School then applied the idea of integration to the study of race and ethnicity, promoting integration through color-blind institutions.[44]

According to Adrian Favell, France entered into a new phase of republicanism in the 1980s as tensions regarding immigration and integration erupted in politics; this new phase of republicanism attempts to balance "diversity and cohesion."[45] However, the state continues to struggle with the "opposition between 'real' French and the 'different' immigrés—what is often discussed as the pervasive logic of 'altértié' (otherness)—which suggests the commitment to diversity is in fact subordinate to the strong substantive idea of what culturally being French should be."[46] In addition to exclusionary policies, the us-(French) versus-them (foreign) rhetoric in national immigration debates sets immigrants at odds with French interests.[47] Despite large numbers of migrants to France, the French state has resisted multiculturalism or even an acknowledgment of the multiethnic makeup of France. France has traditionally had higher immigration rates than other European countries, with immigrants in France serving as an important labor source but also as a means to repopulate the country.[48] Although France attempted to put a stop to labor migration in 1974, the attempts were largely unsuccessful, as instead of workers returning to their countries of origin, many of their spouses and dependents migrated to France as well. As family reunification fueled additional migration, stable ethnic communities formed in France, making clear that the migration of workers and their families predominantly from North Africa was not a temporary phenomenon but rather a long-term issue that France as a nation needed to come to terms with. The term *immigré*, or immigrant, a term largely reserved for immigrants from North or sub-Saharan Africa, came to have negative associations as people in French society came to view immigrants as unassimilable and a threat to the French nation. The term came to be associated with not only immigrants but also their descendants for multiple generations.[49]

In a book focusing on contemporary France from 1974 to the early 2000s, scholar Alec G. Hargreaves examines the 2005 riots in the "banlieues" or poor suburbs of Paris. The word "banlieues" is a racially coded term referring to the densely populated suburbs of Paris with high levels of poverty and consisting of majority Muslim migrants from former French colonies in North and West Africa.

> During the 1980s and 1990s, politicians and public opinion were obsessed with what was widely portrayed as a serious threat to French national identity and social cohesion arising from the settlement of minorities originating in predominantly Islamic countries, mainly former French colonies in North and West Africa. During that period, the central notion in political discourse about those minorities was the need for "integration." To the extent that "integration" was not proceeding at the desired speed, this was commonly blamed on the alleged inability or unwillingness of Muslims to adjust to the cultural norms dominant in France.[50]

Though mainstream French society claimed that Muslims were unassimilable, the lack of integration of Black and Arab Muslim immigrants and their families was really about discrimination (socioeconomic and political factors), not an inability or unwillingness to assimilate.

Challenging dominant discourse on French universalism as an equalizing force, cultural theorist Etienne Balibar asserts that universalism strengthens rather than diminishes racism; in a Machiavellian manner, universalism is used as a tool to employ and naturalize racist practices and institutions by marking those practices as normal.[51] Lisa Lowe also points out the contradictions of national ideologies regarding inclusion. She argues in *Immigrant Acts* that the metropolitan nation needs pluralism economically to be a global empire but needs monoculturalism politically and culturally to sustain national belonging and support state policies of expansion.[52]

In *Citizen/Outsider*, sociologist Jean Beaman examines how France's colonial history frames nonwhite colonial subjects as separate from and less than the implicitly white ideal French citizen. Beaman writes, "Constructing French-ness as white, and French identity as a white one, is part of this racial project, which dates from the construction of the nation itself. French culture is portrayed as an unchanging, homogenous entity."[53] This conception of French-ness as whiteness makes it impossible for immigrants of color and their descen-dants to claim full cultural citizenship in France. According to Beaman, "Ndiaye's (2008) minority paradox, the theory of the simultaneous visibility and invisibility of France's black population, also applies in this middle-class minority population; their visibility is heightened by their presence in pre-dominately white spaces (including elite universities and professional and executive-level offices), but they are invisible because their presence is ignored in mainstream society."[54]

This simultaneous visibility and invisibility also describe the ways that middle- and upper-class Haitian immigrants in France are visible because of their race but invisible because they lack recognition on the national stage.

In France, ethnoracial exclusion largely takes the form of Islamophobia. According to Beaman, "Religion stands in for racial and ethnic difference in a society that refuses to grapple head-on with these differences. Islamophobia is a form of racism—it sees certain individuals as too culturally different to ever be fully accepted as part of the mainstream."[55] Instead of facing racial and cul-tural diversity in France, when North Africans are considered too different from mainstream French identity, Islamophobia allows dominant French nar-ratives to blame Islam for North Africans' apparent inability to assimilate.[56] As we will see in chapter 2, this framing of racism as religious difference tem-porarily renders Christian, Haitian migrants above Muslim, North African migrants in France's ethnoracial hierarchy. While also visibly marked as dif-ferent than the dominant white French identity, Haitians can claim inclusion in France due to their religious affiliation with Frenchness.

Looking beyond cultural integration to economic inequality in France, Alec Hargreaves writes, "If there is a crisis of integration, it is not only cultural and political but also socio-economic in nature."[57] Until recent decades, most immi-grants to France were Catholic. Now, large numbers of immigrants are Mus-lim. In addition to this religious and cultural difference, current Muslim immigrants from Africa experience fewer opportunities for meaningful socio-economic integration than earlier waves of immigrants. Many more recent immigrants from the "Third World" face unemployment and economic restructuring, as opposed to the economic opportunities that were available to European immigrants of the past.

Alec Hargreaves asserts that race does not exist in France and that discrim-ination is cultural rather than based on the idea of biological racism, so there-fore, the discrimination should not be described as racism.[58] In contrast, I argue that racism exists in France, though it manifests differently than in the United

States because of its specific history with regard to colonialism, immigration, and oppressed minorities. Unlike Hargreaves's assessment, racism takes many forms, with biological racism only serving as one of many racist ideologies. Cultural racism certainly exists in France and largely takes the shape of Islamophobia, using religion as a proxy for skin color.

Paris, Ile-de-France. France's national policy on race is legally mandated color blindness. Collecting data on race through any national census is forbidden. This is supposed to ensure color blindness, but it does not translate into an absence of racial tensions, nor does it alter assumptions about which people properly represent the French nation. French law makes it difficult to know exactly how large the Haitian community is in France, but a 2016 survey reports 83,930 Haitian-born people in France. A large number of undocumented Haitian migrants live in Martinique and Guadeloupe, overseas territories of France; however, this study focuses on the Haitians in Paris to parallel the analysis with Boston and Montreal as "Western" metropoles.[59] Mainland France is considerably farther from Haiti than the Caribbean and North American destinations that attract Haitian migrants, but Haiti's history as a former colony of France gives that nation a certain familiarity and appeal to Haitians who have the means to travel there. Over past decades, the Haitian community in France has shifted between moments of great political mobilization and a virtual absence of visible Haitian cultural and political organization.

In reference to the migration of working-class Caribbean women to the Parisian region from 1946 to 1974, Félix F. Germain writes that "despite France's pledge to universal equality, racial and gender differences clearly constrained French citizens. That being said, the migrants were not deterred by racial and gendered barriers. Ambitious and determined Caribbean women found ways to circumvent these obstacles and slowly move up the social ladder."[60]

Fewer Haitians live in the Paris region compared with Montreal or Boston, and as mentioned, France's universalist stance pressures immigrants to assimilate. These two factors combined have led to the creation of a starkly different landscape for the Haitian diaspora there. Haitian community organizations are many in number but seriously lacking in presence. The assimilationist approach to integration within the French national context has led Haitian middle- and upper-class women to navigate cultural inclusion through work on an individual level rather than with the support of diasporic organizations to ease the way into employment and provide networking with other Haitian professionals.

2

Social Ties and Complex
Inclusion in the Nation

Nathalie, a tall, lean, and strikingly beautiful woman with shoulder-length straightened hair and fair skin, was in her late twenties when I met her in 2016. She had moved to Quebec for college after growing up in Haiti. While she initially intended to return to Haiti to work after finishing school, she had built a very comfortable life for herself in Montreal. Nathalie was finishing college around the time of the tragic 2010 earthquake in Port-au-Prince. She had just returned from visiting her family in Haiti for the holidays when the earthquake struck her hometown. Safe in Montreal, Nathalie felt drawn to go back to Haiti and help people who were suffering. Her mother, ever the pragmatist, however, urged Nathalie to finish her studies and to learn a skill that she could apply to help people back in Haiti. This advice prompted Nathalie to continue her studies to earn a master's degree in social work.

Though she initially intended to return to Haiti, Nathalie grew to find ways to help people in Montreal with her newly developed skills. As part of her training in social work, she interned at Maison d'Haïti in Montreal to work with recently immigrated youth from Haiti:

> For the master's, you have an internship for the qualifying year, and then at the end of the master's, you have the other internship that you're doing. So, the first internship I did was at the CAVAC, which is the Crime and Victims Assistance Center. And I *loved* it, because it was a mixture of the law and helping out people who were victims of different kinds of crimes, so I really enjoyed that.

And then, at the end, there's the other half where you have to come up with the internship yourself. You have to come up with a plan and kind of put it in place in a place where you want to do your internship. So, I decided to do my second internship at La Maison d'Haïti in Montreal because I was living in Montreal so it was easier for me to do my internship there. And what I had chosen to do, it was a program where I had eight kids who had lived the quake and I was trying to help them cope with the PTSD or the symptoms that they could have had, trying to use art as a medium to cope with symptoms of PTSD. But I can't use these terms; I couldn't even use "PTSD" because I'm not certified. I'm not a psychologist, I can't diagnose people. So, I can say that I see traits or traces of symptoms that could be related to PTSD and how to use art as a medium to cope with that. So, that's what I did at Maison d'Haïti, and I had to choose an age range, and I went from seven to sixteen.

The combination of Nathalie's personal background of having grown up in Port-au-Prince and her professional skills as a social worker left her uniquely situated to help these children who lived with the trauma of having survived the earthquake. Her transnational ties with family and friends still in Haiti inspired her to help the Haitian community any way she could, even from abroad.

Nathalie's work put her into contact with the Haitian community, allowing her to use her newly developed skills as a social worker to help children process the trauma of the devastating 2010 earthquake that hit Haiti. It also put her into contact with coworkers and clients at the Crime and Victim Assistance Center. Through this work Nathalie became a cultural citizen of Quebec and reaffirmed her Haitian cultural citizenry through her work with the Haitian community in Montreal. She also became part of the fabric of Quebec that situates others, both native-born and immigrant residents of Quebec, with regard to cultural citizenship. Having access to and using the social services that Nathalie provided helped to include residents in the context of Quebec as a nation.

Nathalie was studying in Sherbrooke, another city in Quebec, while living and interning in Montreal. She worked for a number of community organizations aimed at helping youth to stay in school, return to school, or find a job. She worked at these school retention programs while completing her internship and earning her master's degree. When I met Nathalie years later, she was working as a social worker for the government of Quebec in an anglophone division: "We have really good working conditions, although they are trying to change that. But at this moment we really have amazing working conditions. I do a lot of overtime, so the next time I can come in later. It's not always doable and that's when it's sucky that it's so structured as an organization because you kind of have to take it back. So, there are things that are great and there are things that are not so great. But my team is amazing. I get along with my coworkers and my manager is pretty awesome." Nathalie attained a sense of belonging through her government job, where she worked well with and enjoyed the company of her colleagues. Being part of a team, perhaps especially one where she acted as a representative of the government, carved out a place for her within the fabric of Quebecois society.

She also taught and performed Haitian folkloric dance in the evenings and on the weekends. For one of her performances, Nathalie's non-Haitian coworkers, including her boss, attended her Haitian dance show to cheer her on. She told me that it was awkward to have her two worlds meet but that she was extremely grateful for her coworkers' warmth and support. While her identity as a Haitian woman and her strong transnational ties to Haiti spurred her on her career path as a social worker, the relationships she formed in Montreal, including those with her supportive and caring coworkers, anchored her in Quebec and ultimately dissuaded her from returning to Haiti.

Nathalie's experiences illustrate several themes. First, Nathalie demonstrated her agency as a Haitian woman in diaspora to choose a career path suited to her as an individual which also had the capacity to help fellow Haitians, whether in Haiti or abroad. Her internship at Maison d'Haïti shows how this Haitian community center was able to serve as an anchor to help Nathalie in her own professional development while also providing services for recent refugees.[1] Lastly, her employment as a social worker for the government of Quebec put her into contact with many people in the course of her work. Simultaneously, she formed close relationships with coworkers that extend beyond the workplace. The inclusionary nature of her relationship with her fellow government employees clearly situates Nathalie as a valued part of the nation. Even in tense interactions with clients who resented her intervention, those clients' hostility toward her was based on her role as a government employee with the authority to speak on behalf of the nation.

In this chapter I examine the social ties created in the workplace and how those relationships influence Haitian women's positioning in the nation in both inclusionary and exclusionary ways. Even for those who participated in paid labor in Haiti prior to emigrating, employment outside the home post-migration plays a crucial role in that it puts workers into contact with others within the nation. The social ties facilitated by paid labor outside the home place Haitian women within the discourse of the nation through daily, micro-level interactions.

I highlight how social interactions in the workplace situate Haitian women in complex and contradictory relations with both their country of origin and their country of arrival. This chapter follows from the work of scholars who argue that new and established immigrants meet in the workplace.[2] While some scholars take more of an assimilationist approach to understanding how immigrants fit into existing communities, this study examines the role of immigrants, the nation, and work through the lens of cultural citizenship, which contrary to assimilation involves looking at how Haitian immigrant women make and remake their national contexts. Rather than understanding Haitian women migrants as merely acted upon as subjects, this study also views them as active participants in creating the nation. Those social ties in the workplace act to both include and exclude Haitian women in diaspora from national belonging. Factors of race, gender, class, and nation of origin influence how and to what degree these migrants find belonging within the nation. Though all workers experience these phenomena in some fashion, the experiences of Haitian women migrants at the intersection of migration, race, and gender pull into focus the ways in which these processes of social inclusion and exclusion in the nation through work function.

As Aihwa Ong writes in *Flexible Citizenship*, transnational ties between emigrants and the homeland are associated with overseas capital and flexibility.[3] Ong looks at flexible accumulation in terms of both economics and culture, emphasizing that analyses of diaspora frequently miss the opportunity to depict "diasporan subjects as active manipulators of cultural symbols."[4] As seen in this study, Haitian women shape cultural symbols in their workplace interactions. In Ong's study, members of the Chinese diaspora display flexibility in terms of what cultural capital they acquire, enabling them to navigate socially abroad. Ong writes, "Although citizenship is conventionally thought of as based on political rights and participation within a sovereign state, globalization has made economic calculation a major element in diasporan subjects' choice of citizenship, as well as in the ways nation-states redefine immigration laws. I use the term "flexible citizenship" to refer especially to the strategies and effects of mobile managers, technocrats, and professionals seeking to both circumvent *and* benefit from different nation-state regimes by selecting different sites for investments, work, and family relocation."[5] I assert that similar to the migrants from Hong Kong to Northern California in Ong's study, middle- and upper-class Haitian migrants to Montreal, Boston, and Paris are "economically correct in terms of human capital, but culturally incorrect in terms of ethnicity."[6] In this way, Haitians from the middle and upper classes are attractive to Western nations based on their class position and often their professional skills, but simultaneously they remain unattractive as migrants to Western nations because of their racial and ethnic identities.

Through daily interactions in the workplace, Haitian women display agency as they negotiate their race, gender, and status as insiders or outsiders within the nation. Haitian women mediate their workplace social ties in a variety of ways, in some cases rejecting social inclusion because they do not feel they can trust their colleagues, and at other times proudly sticking to their Haitian values of respect regardless of their colleagues' behavior toward them.

I examine the social ties that Haitian women forge in the workplace and argue that these social ties play a crucial role in determining to what extent Haitian women are culturally included in the nation by their own estimation and by the judgment of "insiders."

Social ties among Haitians and between Haitians and non-Haitians shape women's experience of paid labor. In Boston and Montreal, the Haitian communities and their established social networks help many new immigrants find work. In Paris, where Haitian migrants of the middle and upper classes from the Port-au-Prince metropolitan area are more dispersed, such networks are less established.[7] In Montreal, for instance, several of the women I interviewed had interned or worked as consultants for Maison d'Haïti, the central Haitian organization in the city. In Boston, many relayed that they found their first jobs in the city through family networks or Haitian family friends who moved to Boston before them. For instance, Christine described how more established Haitian women in the United States helped recently arrived Haitian women to find low-status, gendered work. It was the only type of work available to them as Black women from a developing country. Christine explained the process of more established Haitian immigrants helping the more recent immigrants find employment:

> We didn't have, I mean, a lot of people that we know tried to help each other, but they didn't have the know-how to help, like . . . they didn't have all these social services back then to help immigrants, first of all, so that was nonexistent. So, it was only Haitians trying to help Haitians, you know? So, my mother, she didn't have too many friends because she didn't have the time. She was always working. She works even Sundays. So, a few other friends of my mother that were working at factories took my sisters and from there, that's how they get to work and then when they start going to the night school, they start getting to know other people and start to say, "Why don't you try to work here instead?" And things like that.

In addition to drawing on networks of Haitians in diaspora, the workplace serves as a site to build social ties with non-Haitians. Social ties in the workplace can lead to supportive relationships and to a sense of inclusion within the nation. At the same time, the workplace can reproduce exclusionary practices, signaling who is a part of the nation and who is rendered an outsider. Sometimes inclusionary and exclusionary practices occur simultaneously, highlighting the fact that they are constantly negotiated through daily interactions. I refer to these practices of simultaneous inclusion and exclusion as "complex" or "contradictory inclusion." Haitian women illuminate these processes of inclusion and exclusion through their workplace experiences in each of the three field sites, drawing attention to the similarities and differences in the ways in which gender and migration manifest across locales.

The social ties that Haitian migrants create in the workplace are important because those ties locate them within the nation. In contrast, Haitian migrants who do not enter the paid workforce outside the home, such as women engaged in informal caring labor, do not have the same opportunities to engage with people outside of their familial social network. Through work outside the home, Haitian women in Montreal come into contact with French Canadians as well as immigrants from all over the world. Similarly, in Boston, Haitian women meet white Americans, African Americans, and a range of immigrants from other places. In Paris, the pattern is much the same with Haitian women who work outside the home coming into contact with a range of people within the nation, including French citizens and immigrants from Africa, Europe, and Asia. This chapter provides ethnographic data to illustrate social ties of inclusion, exclusion, and complex inclusion.

Inclusion

I argue that instances of social inclusion through work signal a sense of belonging within the nation, though this belonging is always mediated by factors of gender, race, and ethnicity. Following a very different trajectory from Nathalie, Micheline's experiences working in Montreal also demonstrate inclusionary social ties that facilitated a sense of belonging within Quebec's national landscape. Micheline, a Haitian dance teacher in her early sixties, traveled to Haiti frequently, where she maintained a network of family and friends and returned to live for periods of time, though she had made Montreal her home continuously for ten years prior to my meeting her. Micheline's story is one of multiple migrations, as she moved to Montreal for schooling, then left her children with her mother in Montreal as she returned to Haiti to work, and then ultimately returned to Montreal to continue her education and establish her dance school.

Micheline had built very close relationships with her non-Haitian dance students. She had been teaching Haitian dance in Montreal for over ten years and had some students who had danced with her that whole time. She shared a level of intimacy with them and referred to them as her children. She regularly kissed each dancer in greeting and stroked their arms and hair while speaking with them.

One day, like so many of the days I spent as a participant observer with Micheline, a tall, awkward white man and a dark-haired white woman, both of whom were in this same dance class two weeks ago when I was there, were sitting near each other in the lobby. The dark-haired woman eagerly flagged Micheline down as we entered the lobby. Micheline greeted the white man by walking up behind him and stroking his head. She verbally greeted the dark-haired woman, who was in the process of writing a check paying Micheline for class. Micheline seemed harried and spoke with them briefly about other students who were away on holiday or would be missing class that night. Micheline stroked the white man's head once more as she urged them to hurry up and move to the classroom, though several minutes still remained until the start of class. Micheline and I walked to the classroom together, and were greeted by a young blonde woman whom I recognized from last time. Micheline walked over to the blonde student and placed a very fond and intentional kiss on the top of her head.

Micheline asked about all their personal lives and gave them advice. In this Francophone-only space, Micheline created an incredibly warm and familial atmosphere for herself and her students. Montreal became a home where she was surrounded by both blood and chosen family, much of which came in the form of her predominantly French-Canadian dance students, whom she clearly adored.

For Micheline, her social ties with her French-Canadian dance students helped her to make a living. In teaching them Haitian dance, she displayed her expertise about Haitian culture. Perhaps paradoxically, her status as Haitian and therefore an outsider brought her into contact with French Canadians who actively sought to learn about a culture other than their own. Like ethnic food or craft vendors, Micheline's ethnic identity and knowledge of folkloric dance enable her to turn her "difference" into a marketable commodity that offers entry to the larger community.

Unlike Nathalie, who had close relationships with peers in her workplace, Micheline's work-based social ties were wrapped up in consumerism, as her students paid her to perform a service. Though in some ways Micheline's work reproduces colonial tropes of white Westerners seeking to learn more about an "exotic" Other, Micheline also exercises agency in that she works for herself and sets the terms under which she shares her culture.[8] While kind and effusive, she always taught with authority, and her students showed deference to her during classes. Through her work, Micheline took on a mothering role in which she was loving but firm, adhering to stereotypes of what mothering entails in both Haitian and Canadian culture and explicitly positioning herself as a mother to her white, French-Canadian students. Whether intentionally or not, Micheline's adoption of the mothering role resonates with a long history of women of color in child-rearing roles for white families due to the structuring of the global political economy that designates women of color in caring labor roles for white Westerners as a form of subordinate inclusion.

Martine, a Haitian woman in her thirties with two young children, also found that her relationships at work helped her to feel that she belonged in Quebec. For Martine, a child psychoeducation specialist, her relationship with her coworkers made her feel that she had found her place in Montreal.

When I was sick at my old job, no one came to see me. In this job, they came to my house, two of them came to see me and they brought flowers from the whole team. They put money together and bought a big basket. When I returned to the office, they had left a lot of notes on my desk saying they had missed me. I had only been there for one year. I hadn't yet developed a relationship with them, but they have good values there. I feel good that no one talks about the others. It's not a negative environment where everyone whines. They are positive. Sometimes they're not happy. They make jokes. Some of my colleagues make jewelry; they have hobbies. They do projects together. It's for that reason that I say I've found my place, a place where my values and competencies are in agreement.

NC: And now you have friends from work whom you see outside of work? What do you do together?
M: Yes, there are three of us. One quit, but we still see her. We meet for lunch. We love to eat. One of us says that we've found a new restaurant and we go try it together. When we arrive, we talk about everything, family . . . [laughter] we talk about everything, about work, but not too much about work. We mostly talk about life.

While not the case at her previous place of employment, Martine reported a strong sense of social inclusion at her current place of work at the time of the interview. She pointed to the fact that her coworkers expressed concern for her during her illness as a clear sign of her inclusion. For Martine, those social ties extended beyond the workplace, with her going out to eat regularly with a small group of colleagues. Her relationship with these colleagues gave her a sense of belonging in Montreal.

In Boston, Marjorie also experienced social inclusion through her work, though Marjorie's sense of belonging within the nation came not from her coworkers, but from government officials with whom she came into contact through work. In her early sixties, Marjorie was a tall woman with medium brown skin and short, dark brown hair who worked for a nonprofit providing social services for the Haitian community in Boston. Marjorie has won awards and accolades from the city of Boston for her work with vulnerable populations in the area. She told me that she was always embarrassed to receive awards but that she had received recognition from both the mayor and the governor for her work. Though she works predominantly with Haitians, her work was recognized by Americans beyond the Haitian community. Marjorie explained:

The mayor gave me an award. It was in the paper; the *Boston Globe* wanted to do an interview with me. At that time, we had Governor Mitt Romney. . . .

My daughter always says, "I don't know why you have all those plaques and citations." I think I probably have twenty-five or something, or thirty. I've got from the House of Representatives, I've got from the Senate, I've got them from Governor Mitt Romney, from Governor Deval Patrick, I think I've got three things from Mayor Menino. But I never display them. They are all in a box in the corner of my house. Because I told people I don't want it. They know me so well now that if they are giving me something they don't tell me that they are giving me anything until I'm sitting in the room and they call my name and I have to get up. Even my job here. They gave me something and I didn't have a clue.

NC: Why don't you want the recognition?
M: I'm not doing it for anything. I don't know.

Marjorie's recognition for her work by state officials did not erase deeply entrenched racial tensions and hierarchies in the city, but it explicitly situated Marjorie and her work within the discourse of the nation.

In addition to her recognition for the social services she provides, Marjorie also supervised social work interns, most of whom were non-Haitian Americans in their twenties. Through this supervision, she plays a role in shaping the next generation of social workers who will work in a range of positions both inside and outside the Haitian community. Marjorie's work gave her a sense of purpose that rooted her within the Haitian community of Boston, and therefore within the larger landscape of the city and the United States as a nation.

Bernadette, an affable and verbose elderly woman, described work in conjunction with freedom and independence, as well as the opportunity to assume responsibility in a management capacity in the workplace. I met with Bernadette in the dark living room of her home in the suburbs of Boston. She had light skin and white hair pulled back, and she explained that her ailing husband was in the bedroom. She moved slowly but was still mobile and very mentally acute. While I was at her home, a dark-skinned Haitian woman we both knew came in to perform domestic labor. This second woman did not speak any English.

Bernadette initially immigrated to New York in the late 1960s at the age of eighteen, soon after marrying her husband. Bernadette's first husband, a man several years her elder, was controlling and abusive. He did everything he could to prevent her from keeping a job or pursuing her education. Bernadette refused to assume the role of a submissive young bride and felt strongly about working and making her own money in the United States.

For Bernadette, whose experiences moving to New York initially before moving to Boston working on an assembly line not only granted her some degree of financial independence but also expanded her very limited social circle against the wishes of her controlling husband. Bernadette explained how hard it was for her to send for her sister to come to New York to join her: "For a few months, because she could not stay because of him. So, I had to struggle to get some money to send to her. I couldn't find no money. I tried to ask people for money, because I could not get the money. And he could have given me money to get all of them to come. But like I told you, he did not want people to be around me. That's the controlling. I did it anyway."

Bernadette explained that she did not have any friends in the United States when she initially migrated to live with her husband but that she was able to meet some people through work:

Yes, from work. I'd get some friends, I'd talk to them. A couple of them came to my house. . . . And you can call, we talked . . .

And when I was working, there was a lot of Spanish people, I was around a lot of Spanish people, and they were speaking Spanish. Because I knew a couple words of Spanish. And they thought that I was Spanish. My god, you know. And sometimes they talk together; they don't want me to hear what they were saying because they thought that I understand that. And yeah, but I had a good time going to work. Because there are people, friends. And I find some Haitian friend, also. We talk, we laugh. Yeah, so you know, it was really good. That's why you know.

Though her husband tried to isolate her from friends and family when she migrated from Haiti, through work she was able to carve out a social space for herself outside of her relationship with him. Her friends from work counseled her at one point, giving her advice about how to handle the situation with her abusive husband. According to Nancy Foner, "working outside the home also broadens migrant women's social horizons and enhances their sense of independence."[9] After a particularly violent incident in which her husband attacked her with a baseball bat, Bernadette returned to Haiti, filed divorce papers, and then moved to Boston with the help of family friends. She lived and worked in Boston for decades, where she received job training to perform data entry and was free to work without her ex-husband controlling her every move.

In Paris, it was so common for immigrants to be the only Haitians working in any given environment that it was the norm, and therefore not notable. Nadia, a short, middle-aged Haitian woman with medium-brown skin and straightened hair who lived just outside Paris, described having such a close relationship with one of her white French coworkers that she was like an aunt to his children and he was like an uncle to hers. I observed Nadia interact with another white French woman whom Nadia introduced to me as one of her old colleagues.

Nadia lived in a quiet complex of slightly dated attached houses at the far end of her suburban town. There is a wealth of greenery around the complex, including a river, a prairie, and many mature trees. After our interview concluded, Nadia offered to walk me part of the way back to the train station, taking a different route than the one I had followed on my way there. Instead of returning to the street, she walked down a steep grassy hill toward the river. We walked through the prairie alongside the river, which was peaceful and absolutely beautiful. After walking for a few minutes, we came upon groups of people picnicking and grilling food. One woman called out loudly to Nadia, who immediately stopped in her tracks with surprise before happily walking over to greet her, with me in tow. She told me that the woman, a white French woman from a small town in the south of France, was one of her old colleagues. They embraced warmly with emphatic kisses and a big hug. Nadia commented on the woman's tan, joking that she was almost as dark as her now. They talked about their vacations, and the woman introduced us to her sister. Nadia's social inclusion with her coworkers showed both through her interview and through my observations of her interacting with this old colleague so familiarly.

Each of these examples illustrates how Haitian women can experience social inclusion through paid labor. In some cases, that inclusion comes in the form of developing supportive relationships with colleagues. In other instances, such as Marjorie's, inclusion comes in the form of formal recognition at the level of the state. Haitian women belong within the nation differently from native-born residents because they have affiliations and allegiances overseas, the manifestations of their "flexible citizenship."[10] The state recognition for Marjorie's work is a meaningful step toward cultural inclusion and national belonging on a symbolic level, though it remains to be seen how the symbolic recognition translates to support in tangible or affective ways.

A handful of Haitian women in this study worked for international organizations that drew them into contact not only with those within the nation but with a transnational community. Tamara, a tall, middle-aged woman with light skin dusted with freckles, worked for the United Nations in Paris after leaving Haiti. During her time with the United Nations, she lived in Africa from 1996 to 2011, dwelling in Sierra Leone, the Central African Republic, and Cote d'Ivoire. During her time in Africa, her children remained in Paris with her husband. When asked if she had a lot of friends from her time in Africa, Tamara responded, "Mostly we communicate on Facebook. I keep in contact with colleagues who became friends. We have things in common. They are from all over the world. French, Moroccan, Russian, Egyptian, American, et cetera." While work for many Haitian women leads to some degree of inclusion in their new national context, upon moving to France, Tamara's work with the United Nations put her in contact with a global community of expats, fostering a different sort of inclusion through paid labor that is not explicitly tied to a singular national context.

Exclusion

While the workplace brings many together in a way that fosters inclusion, it can also serve as a site where the limits of inclusion become clear. Gina, a Haitian woman in her late twenties to early thirties who moved to Quebec in elementary school, described an experience of blatant racism and social exclusion in the workplace. Gina had dark brown skin and natural black hair. She worked as a nurse in one of the hospitals in Montreal. Gina said,

> When I started working, I was nineteen or twenty years old. I encountered blatant racism, like nurses who didn't want to take my report at the end of my shift because they said they didn't understand my accent. I had been living there since I was seven years old! In France I was told that I speak with a Quebecois accent, but knew that it wasn't because of my accent, it was because of who I am. . . . Outside of work this group of nurses were friends, and when they invited each other to do things, one of them asked if they weren't going to invite me too. The woman responded, "No, her color will dirty my spa."
> . . .
> A nurse came to see me outside of work, and she told me, "Gina, I don't like Black people, but I like you very much." Ever since I've been in Quebec I've been fucked by your government and yet I don't understand these white people. She looked at me while I searched for an answer, and to her I was being aggressive because in her mind she was paying me a compliment.

Sometimes the limits of inclusion come in the form of overt hostilities, but more frequently Haitian women experienced subtler forms of social exclusion in the workplace that led to mistrust of their non-Haitian colleagues. Farah is a tall, dark-skinned woman with shoulder-length straightened hair. She wears glasses and has a slight gap between her front teeth. She works part-time as an event coordinator for a company in Montreal and part-time as a self-employed fitness coach. Farah was cordial with her coworkers after migrating to Montreal in the early 2000s but never fully trusted them.

Farah's mistrust of her coworkers in Montreal stands in stark contrast to the way she described her mother's sense of inclusion in the workplace in Haiti. When asked if her mother worked in Haiti, Farah replied,

Yes, my mother worked in Haiti all her life. She worked in the public sector. She worked there for thirty-five years, and now she is retired.

NC: Did she like this work?
F: Yes, she loved it because she had a lot of friends. It was like a second family. Many, if not all, of her best friends worked there with her, so she really loved it.

Farah described a couple of jobs in Haiti that she held after university that she did not like, but the last position she held was her "dream job" with a marketing agency that she only left in order to migrate to Canada because of security concerns in Haiti. At the marketing agency she made only a fraction of her previous salary, but she accepted the position because she was interested in the work: "In reality, I really love marketing. And since I didn't make a lot of money, they bought me a car. It's really interactive, like you have contact with artists, you have contact with the radio, there are events. And you take care of clients. How can I say this ... you have responsibilities. You feel valued. I really loved it there." When asked if she got along with her colleagues at the marketing agency, Farah replied, "Oh yeah, it was amazing. It was my dream job."

After migrating to Montreal, Farah has a decidedly different relationship with her coworkers than she and her mother experienced while living in Haiti. The following interview excerpt comes from Farah describing her work with the government of Montreal:

NC: And did you make good friends with any of the other people [at work]?
F: Not really, because I didn't trust them, not really. What's the point to be friends with someone you don't trust? I say hi, we can tell jokes, but I don't consider them my friends.
. . .
If you are in an office, the Blacks or the immigrants are not really friends with the other ones, while the other ones, they don't work actually, they just pass the whole day talking about boring stuff. So, it was like this at the government, the immigrants for example, I didn't have Haitians, but there were many people from Algeria, Morocco. They are the ones who are working and you don't see them joke a lot. But the Quebecois from nine to five are always talking about something [boring like the weather].
They don't work. But us, if we don't work, it's like, "Look at them, they are lazy." Or if you are in the process of talking, they'll say weird things like, "Why aren't you working?" So, you feel like you have to work, while they can do whatever they want to do.

Farah explains that the norm was for her and the other Black and immigrant employees to work diligently while the white Quebecois employees spend a lot of time chatting and wasting time. However, if one of the employees of color acted in a way similar to the white employees, racial stereotypes of Blacks being lazy would be used against them. Farah further described the climate of racialized surveillance in her workplace: "So, it's subtle, but it's like they're controlling.... Always controlling. That's why I wasn't friends with them, because I don't like people controlling me. So, you always feel that they are [always watching,] is she laughing, is she smiling, is she on the internet? Talking on the phone? Always someone, like it was ridiculous. But they were always talking about boring stuff. It's really annoying. If it's your boss, okay. Your boss can watch you, but when it's other employees watching you it's annoying."

Farah relayed hearing her coworkers talk behind each other's backs and gossip about banal topics when they were supposed to be working, but she was afraid that if she was ever caught engaging in the same behavior, they would report her for not performing her work up to standard. She also worried that her coworkers were trying to pump her for information to find something to use against her at a later time, a concern expressed by several women I interviewed in Montreal. Though the origin of these suspicions remains unclear, they presumably stem from contrasts between work culture in Haiti and in Canada, where in Haiti colleagues frequently maintain more of a professional distance and in Canada colleagues engage as if they were close friends who feel comfortable asking details about each other's lives, demanding a sort of intimacy in the workplace that makes some Haitian migrants uncomfortable.

Farah also explains that the main issue is with French-speaking Quebecois instead of their minority anglophone counterparts: "Here you have the Quebecois but you have also the Anglophone; they are different. And still, it's like there's a separation between the two, like the Anglophones are cool with you, no racism. But the Quebecois who mostly speak French, they're worse. So, I can deal better with the Anglophones. It's their mentality, I think. It's a different mentality. It's really the worst. They want to know what's happening about you but it's not because they are interested or care; they are just building like a case against you that they will use later." Farah's account of trouble with francophone Quebecois colleagues speaks to the tension between those who seek to maintain Quebecois culture and those who do not fit neatly into that traditional idea of what it means to belong in Quebec.

In Boston, Josette, a woman in her late thirties who left Haiti following the 2010 earthquake, reported having a similar relationship to her colleagues as Farah in Montreal. Josette had dark-brown skin and shoulder-length straightened hair always pulled back in a tight, low bun. Though she often had a quiet and almost demure manner in the office, Josette laughed openly and joked with me when we spent time together outside of work. Josette worked for a nonprofit in a new office building just outside Boston. Josette admitted that although her coworkers were nice, she did not have close relationships with any of them. In addition to Josette's self-reporting on her relationship with colleagues, my participant observation spending time with her at her place of work revealed that Josette was frequently ignored or overlooked by white colleagues who enthusiastically greeted each other in the halls of her Boston office. Josette was the only Haitian and one of very few people of color in a building of about 300 employees. Josette complained that the fake niceties that were so common in her office were culturally incompatible with her respectful but honest Haitian values. Josette explained that her job in Boston is a considerable demotion from what she had been doing for work in Haiti: "Let me tell you something: when I started working here, I started working as an administrative assistant, which was not even a downgrade. It was lower than that. Since then, I've had to prove myself and I guess I had to work twice or three times harder than anyone else because when you're from a country that everyone has a conception of, they second-guess everything that you do, even when you've proven that you can do the work." Here Josette explained differences in respect and workplace etiquette as experienced through her work:

> Everyone here will tell you that Josette will tell you right in your face what's what. To me, that's the way I have been raised. And I always tell everyone that if there's something that you need to talk to me about, I would really appreciate it if you would have the courage to just come and talk to me, because I'm not going to guess it. I'm not going to care; I'm sorry. In a work environment you would think that everyone is adult enough to talk but it isn't so. I think that's the culture here; people are really hypocrites. Everyone wants to be nice to everyone, even if they hate the person. But the thing is that you don't have to like someone to work with the person, you just have to respect the person. As long as there is respect, that's all that matters. Liking someone and everything else is not important.
>
> I remember here [at work] going into the restroom and someone made a comment about something that I was wearing. She said "Oh my God, I really like that! That's a really cool shirt," or something like that. The shirt had a hole in it. Or was it my hair or something? They made a comment about it and it was so strange—when I looked, it was because I had something that was really wrong. So, I realize that here, people, when they don't have the courage to say something, they pretend to joke about it. So that's really different. That's why I can't really consider here home. It's different.

For Josette, the polite way for her colleague to respond would be to openly tell her that there was something wrong with her appearance, instead of complimenting her as a backhanded way of drawing attention to the issue. Josette, and many of the other Haitian women in this study, viewed directness as the most appropriate behavior in the workplace instead of the dominant norms of politeness that require indirect communication.

Numerous factors influence Haitian women's ability to integrate fully into the workplace in Canada, France, and the United States. Contrary to the Pakistani women in Toronto in Lalaie Ameeriar's study, aspects of Haitian women's "bodily comportment," such as style of dress, closely resemble the Canadian norm.[11] Thus, the type of clothing that Haitian women typically wear does not stand out and immediately marks them as Other, making Haitian women appear more able to assimilate into Canadian workplace culture.

The French language also plays an important role in determining who is considered a part of the nation in Quebec and France. In Quebec, the fact that middle- and upper-class Haitians speak French as a native tongue enables this segment of the Haitian population to present themselves as migrants who will bolster Quebec's French identity. In fact, Haitians with whom I spoke in Montreal took great pride in the fact that they spoke a more proper form of French than the Quebecois.

Alternately, skin color forever marks Haitians in Quebec as outside of the white French-Canadian ethnicity, rendering them permanently as outsiders. Similarly, skin color marks Haitian women as Other in France, though Western dress signals Haitians as more a part of the French national identity than Muslim immigrants from North Africa and the Middle East, who typically wear clothing that easily marks them as Other.

In Boston, at first glance Haitians resemble African Americans, calling to mind a long history of racial oppression and racial tensions that are central to the United States' national identity. Being lumped together with African Americans means that Haitians may appear to be insiders in the sense that African Americans have been a part of the United States since its inception, but outsiders in that African Americans are considered to be outside of dominant white American identity.[12] Since dress renders Haitians largely indistinguishable from African Americans, language and accent serve as more critical markers of Haitian immigrants' status as outsiders.

Rather than attempting to shed all signs of cultural difference to assimilate in the workplace, many of the Haitians I interviewed spoke of their Haitian values, such as respect, with pride. Instead of trying to hide or minimize their Haitian values, these women reported that they bring those values with them into the workplace and conduct themselves according to those values regardless of the behavior of those around them. As Josette noted, "As long as there is respect, that's all that matters."

As the above examples demonstrate, social exclusion in the workplace can take many forms, from open racial hostility to a quiet misalignment of cultural values. Open hostility certainly occurs, as in the case of Gina's coworker suggesting that her black skin would dirty the water of her spa; however, it was much more common for the Haitian women with whom I spoke to report a much subtler form of social exclusion in the workplace, as in the examples of Farah and Josette. Race and nation of origin exist as intertwined factors that contribute to patterns of inclusion and exclusion. Though racial exclusion varied greatly between Montreal and Boston during the 1960s and 1970s, contemporary patterns of exclusion in Boston and Montreal, both cities a part of nations that embrace multicultural ideology, appear remarkably similar, as illustrated in the examples of Farah and Josette above.

Complex Inclusion

The workplace can at times simultaneously serve as a site of inclusion and exclusion. Nathalie explained the complicated relationship she had with her previous employer. She worked hard to earn her master's degree and expected that to count in her favor in the workplace; however, her employer at the community organization where she worked had a mentality that it didn't matter if someone had a PhD because they still did not know any better than she did. She valued years of experience on the job over degrees. When I asked Nathalie if she liked her coworkers at that job or not, she responded,

> Sure. [laughter] Well, it's because they had that, a lot of them had that [attitude]. There was one I loved, she's amazing, but there were two others, I don't know. They also had that mentality that I came later, they had been working at the community organization a lot longer than I had, they were older than I was, but I had the master's degree and they didn't. I had the lived experience in Haiti; they didn't. Well, I mean it doesn't really matter, you can have any other kind of life experience, but they weren't recognizing what I was bringing to the table as such.

Nathalie expressed frustration that her qualifications and experience living in Haiti were not valued in this workplace. She also strongly valued structure and felt that it was an important contribution she could make to the children the organization served. She explained:

> And I'm very organized and a perfectionist, and they were kind of like, "Oh, well, we've been doing this for a lot longer and what you're trying to do isn't going to work with them." But I was like, "These kids, they need structure." And it was like, "Oh, well, you just came in. We'll try your way, but it won't work." Well, if you try my way but you're already saying it won't work, then yes, definitely, it won't work. You're kind of setting me up for failure. So, it was kind of a thing like that. I was a little bummed out because every time I tried to bring something up it was like, "Yeah okay, we'll try but it won't work. You

don't know these kids. We know these kids." I was like, "But I have been working here for a while now; I kind of understand.

I've also done research about it, I also have a master's degree, so I'm a professional social worker, and they need a certain kind of structure. If we can't as the organization give them some kind of structure, then they are going to be disorganized in every aspect of their lives. And they are already disorganized! So how are we helping them going forward if we're not doing something?" And so, anyway. It wasn't for me. It was no longer for me.

This conversation with Nathalie illustrates the complicated relationship she had with her coworkers that at times included her and other times left her feeling marginalized. On the one hand, she was in contact with others in the nation and forming relationships; on the other hand, she felt devalued in those relationships because she was from Haiti.

Gladys, a partially retired nurse in her late sixties, described her work environment in Montreal as extremely diverse, offering her the opportunity to strategize with immigrants from other places about how best to deal with racism and social exclusion in the workplace. The following is an excerpt from my field notes:

Gladys called me the day before to reschedule our meeting from earlier in the day. She said that there was an emergency and she had to be at the hospital, but insisted that she could meet me at 4 P.M. because she could easily walk over from the hospital. [I mistakenly thought she meant that she was seeing a sick family member and was hesitant to do the interview while she was dealing with a family emergency, but I gave in to her insistence.] During our talk I learned that she is a retired nurse, but that she is still called in sometimes to do shifts at the hospital when they are short-staffed. She worked a full day, eight to four, before walking over to meet me for the interview, and she confided that it was a particularly tiring day.

Gladys is curvy and short in stature, with straightened gray hair pulled back in a tight ponytail. She bought a coffee and a slice of a galette de roi, which she offered to share with me. She expressed that she was happy to speak in French or English, as she has worked in an all-anglophone environment for over forty years. At the start of our meeting, she seemed a bit guarded, but after a few minutes she was very warm and extremely talkative.

As we got up to leave, Gladys stopped at a table close to the door to dig through one of her two bags for her bus pass. She explained that she no longer has her own locker at the hospital since she is technically retired, so she doesn't leave her bus pass in her coat while she's working. I asked how frequently she is called in to work since she is retired, and she replied that initially they called her to take shifts all the time because a change in administration made it challenging to hire nurses as needed, but she told them that they needed to call her less.

Gladys explained the multicultural atmosphere in the anglophone hospital where she spent most of her career:

> Here in Montreal, there are lots of immigrants and you work with a lot of immigrants. I remember sometimes when we had meetings I thought, "Oh my God, this is like the United Nations!" You have them from Asia, Europe, people from everywhere. You know all those nurses sitting there from everywhere. You have the European championship for soccer—don't go trying to change the channel when you're in the cafeteria, because we're all sitting there and we all know the game. You are constantly in relationship with other immigrants. That doesn't mean that they're not racist toward you, but we have a certain accommodation between us. Because we know we're immigrants, we know what we're going through, and so you have a bit of complicity between you. So, I go there, talk to a guy, he's from Iran, but we usually talk about our experience and sometimes what happens to me. We exchange sometimes things that hurt [him], and I say, "Okay, ignore them." We give each other pointers also. Being an immigrant does that to you.

While Gladys and her coworkers experienced discrimination from Canadians in the workplace, work also provided an environment where immigrants from different backgrounds interacted with each other and shared survival strategies. As Ong notes in the case of Malaysian women in the workplace, daily contact did not erase racial hostilities between minority groups in Gladys's work environment. As Gladys states in the quote above, "That doesn't mean that they're not racist toward you, but we have a certain accommodation between us." Gladys experienced racial slights from white Quebecers and even from other non-white immigrants. Their proximity in the workplace did not resolve all issues of racial discrimination, but it did put Gladys and her Iranian coworker into a position where they could strategically work together to help each other cope with racism from the dominant racial group. Gladys as a Haitian migrant and her coworker as an Iranian migrant are in close proximity "not only spatially but also because of parallel cultural experience."[13] They undergo a coming-together based on their shared experience of living on the margins of dominant society.

Growing up in Haiti, now-retired nurse Guerda was the fifth child in a family of eight. She described herself as a rowdy and sassy child, traits that did not diminish as she aged. Her mother was a teacher and her father a lawyer. Her father became involved in politics in Haiti in the late 1950s and was ultimately arrested and killed.

Guerda completed high school and vocational school in Haiti. She wanted to pursue kinesiology or physiotherapy but did not have a lot of money, and those educational paths were too expensive. Instead, she decided to complete a three-year training to become a nurse because that was a more affordable option. While Guerda was completing her studies, there was a large student strike and government crackdown that led her to fear for her safety because of her association with her late father. Guerda completed her studies, got married, and spent some time in New York with her husband before moving to Montreal when her husband found a job there. She was the first in her family to leave Haitian soil.

Guerda entered a hostile workplace in Montreal in the 1970s where her coworkers did not want to interact with her. Over time she developed relationships with them, and they came to trust and like her. Initially they ignored her, refusing to greet her when she joined the team at work. This social exclusion eventually gave way as Guerda and her colleagues grew to know each other over years spent working side by side.

In *Spirits of Resistance and Capitalist Discipline*, Aihwa Ong briefly notes that through work in factories, young Malaysian women come into contact with other Malaysians and with non-Malays.[14] Ong asserts that this daily contact with coworkers and friends of other ethnicities did not "inevitably lead to a political movement which would replace ethnic hostilities with class consciousness."[15] In agreement with Ong's assertion that daily contact in the workplace will not necessarily lead to solidarity among workers and the dissolution of racial and ethnic disparities, I unpack what does occur through those daily interactions. I argue that the relationships formed in the workplace are central to understanding how migrants become situated within their new host nation because of the ways in which daily workplace interactions influence who feels a sense of national belonging and to what extent.

Among those in Montreal, several reported that working in an anglophone environment had a completely different feel than a francophone environment. For instance, Monique was a doctor by training and had practiced in Haiti for years before migrating to Montreal following the 2010 earthquake. She continued to work as a researcher in the medical field, though she did not acquire her Canadian accreditations to practice medicine in Montreal. In an anglophone medical setting, all the staff referred to her as "doctor" out of respect, as her many years of training and practice as a doctor in Haiti informed her ability to carry out her job as a researcher. However, Monique told me that she previously worked in a francophone environment in Montreal where they would never have referred to her as "doctor" because of a strict adherence to rules and requirements that she had not met in Canada. She described the anglophone environment as much warmer and more relaxed in comparison to the rigidly hierarchical environment in her francophone workplace. Like Farah, Monique found it easier to feel a sense of inclusion with anglophone colleagues than in French-speaking Quebecois workplaces. Based on reports from participants in Montreal, the francophone workplaces seem to mirror France's intensely bureaucratic tendencies, perhaps in an effort to maintain similarities between French-Canadian culture and French culture.

Maintaining steady transnational ties and a strong sense of her Haitian identity could bolster Monique when dealing with downward mobility and lack of respect for her training in the workplace. While refusing to acknowledge her training as a doctor in francophone medical spaces in Montreal could be seen as an attempt to exclude Monique from certain privileges as well as socially in her work environment, maintaining deep connections to Haiti, including a strong desire to return to Haiti one day, could protect Monique from internalizing the disrespect and social exclusion experienced in her francophone work environment. I term Monique's experience as "complex inclusion" because even in the anglophone workplace, she experienced downward mobility from her previous status as a licensed medical doctor. The friendliness of her anglophone colleagues did not prevent Monique from experiencing marginalization, because her medical training was considered inferior because she was Haitian and did not complete her training in Canada, even though she completed some of her training in the United States.

Though several Haitian women reported a marked difference between anglophone and francophone spaces in Montreal, the observed distinction was not a steadfast rule, as seen in the example of Micheline above. Additionally, though each of the examples of complex inclusion provided here happen to come from Montreal, complex inclusion is not a uniquely Quebecois practice; these examples merely illustrate the process most clearly.

While simultaneously experiencing inclusion and exclusion within their new national contexts, most Haitian women with whom I spoke also maintain rich relationships with Haiti and other sites of the Haitian diaspora. As suggested by Mary Waters, holding onto one's identity and social status in Haiti may help to lessen the blow of social exclusion in the forms of racism and xenophobia in their new homes.[16] Though working to create a place for themselves within their new national contexts, knowing that they already belong within the Haitian national context serves as a source of pride and security. This is especially true given the class status of the women in this study within Haitian society. As members of the middle and upper classes in Haiti, these women can find some comfort in the memory of social superiority when experiencing downward mobility and racism in their new homes.

Conclusion

Relationships within the workplace function in contradictory ways, marking Haitian women as both insiders and outsiders in terms of cultural citizenship, depending on context. Through these daily interactions, Haitian women are situated and situate themselves as part of the national context within which they live and work. As part of the Haitian diaspora, Haitians abroad are by nature part of multiple national contexts simultaneously. For some, their status as members of the Haitian nation facilitates their entry into the workforce in their new national contexts by way of Haitian diasporic communities. The social ties formed and maintained through Haitian diasporic communities in Boston and Montreal support members of the Haitian nation in their entry into the American and Quebecois/Canadian nations, respectively.

Social ties within the workplace between Haitians and non-Haitians then further work to situate Haitian women within the context of the nation by providing opportunities for daily interactions through which national inclusion and exclusion are formed. As chapter 6 will explore, the social ties forged in the workplace and the social ties that connect women to Haiti and its diasporic communities allow Haitian women to engage in the cultural work of re-creating and maintaining multiple national contexts.

3

Gendered Race and Ethnicity Across Borders

During an interview on a cold winter morning in 2016 in the living room of her home, a bright and sunny space, Guerda reflected on her entry into Quebec's workforce as a Black woman in the 1970s:

> I moved [to Quebec] in the 1970s and it was very difficult for Black women, very difficult. We were expected to stay in our low-level jobs and not advance. There was this condescendence. I remember when I arrived at the hospital for my job and they all knew that I was the new hire, but no one would even look at me. I was the only Black person there. So, I loudly said, "My name is Guerda. I am a part of your team now." A few years later, when they had come to trust me, they told me that they were not very happy that I had started working with them because they were not used to working with Black people.

Guerda forcefully inserted herself into her new work team, boldly introducing herself and stating her position as if daring her new coworkers to challenge her right to be there.

In Montreal during the Quiet Revolution, Haitian migrants met a type of anti-Black racist resistance that was deeply grounded in xenophobic fears of outsiders diluting the prized French-Canadian ethnic identity. This xenophobia no doubt carried with it racist undertones, given that the ocular component of race allows one to differentiate between racial "insiders" and "outsiders." Quebec provides an example of a dominant native ethnic group (French-Canadian) attempting to protect itself from outside threats. As seen in the example above, Haitian women came face to face with French-Canadian racism when attempting to integrate in the workplace. Guerda's French-Canadian colleagues refused to greet her because they were uncomfortable and unhappy having to work with a Black woman. Guerda challenged their quiet xenophobia and anti-Black racism by boldly introducing herself to the silent room and making a show of acting overly polite and cordial in the face of their silent treatment. Through her continued work alongside these colleagues, she eventually became integrated to the point where they felt comfortable verbalizing their earlier misgivings. Guerda asserted her belonging within the nation, her cultural citizenship, through her interactions with colleagues in the workplace.

I investigate shifts in racial and ethnic identity for Haitian women as they participate in multiple national contexts. Haitian women's diverse experiences highlight some of the ways in which the workplace serves as a site where categories of race and ethnicity are established and maintained through daily interactions. These categories of race and ethnicity situate Haitian women within the context of the nation of arrival, indicating varying levels of belonging within the nation in relation to people of other racial and ethnic groups.[1] Later in this chapter I also include the experiences of women who work for international organizations upon migrating, as that professional experience further complicates dynamics of race, nation, and belonging.

We must understand the experiences of Haitian women with regard to race and ethnicity in each of these locales as shaped by the historical contexts of each setting. Though all three countries can be considered white supremacist nations, the particularities of how racism manifests differs from place to place. In Boston, early immigrants found themselves in the midst of a struggle over desegregation, part of a long history of the "afterlife of slavery" and forced segregation in the United States.[2] That racial history shaped the experiences of Haitian migrants as they worked to find their place within a raced social, political, and economic hierarchy. Haitians in Montreal around this same time faced a strikingly different landscape. Racism certainly existed in the Montreal context as well, but it was shaped by the history of Quebec's ethnic identity and anxieties over protecting and maintaining a uniquely Quebecois ethnic identity. Compared with Boston, the racism faced by Haitians in Quebec was much more subtle, though still pervasive. Quebec did not carry the same history of slavery and segregation, which means that racism developed quite differently in Quebec than in the United States.

Lastly, France's long imperial history has shaped the nation's deeply entrenched racist ideologies. As an imperial metropole, Paris has long attracted migrants from previous colonies. Haiti's fight for independence fades into more distant history when compared with the more recent fight for Algerian independence. Since Haitians migrated to France in much smaller numbers, they were able to integrate with more ease in some ways than if Haitians had a larger presence on the national stage. As discussed in chapter 1, many contemporary French citizens generally view North African immigrants as unable to assimilate and a threat to the nation. Experiences of middle- and upper-class Haitian migrants shed light on the shifting meanings associated with racial and ethnic identity and the ways in which those meanings influence daily life. Haitians in Paris are dispersed enough that they do not garner much national attention as a group, though literature on Black Europe points to anti-Black racism regardless of class or migration status.

Blackness, Haitianness, Race, and Ethnicity

First Wave of Migration: Racial Contexts

As race is a socially constructed category, the ways in which race is socially constructed in Haiti differ from the social construction of race in the United States, Canada, and France.[3] In Haiti, race and class function as interconnected categories that make up colorism, with lighter-skinned Haitians tending to occupy positions of power and membership in the higher socioeconomic classes.[4] Perhaps as a result of the strong correlation between race and class in Haiti, race serves as a much more fluid category in Haiti than in the United States. For instance, a person's race in Haiti may change based on his or her social and economic situation, rather than being fixed based on one's skin color. When moving to the United States, however, Haitians face much less flexible racial categories that impact their interpersonal relations.[5]

In Montreal, the first wave of Haitian migrants encountered issues of social integration. The government opened its borders to Haitian migrants of a certain class because Quebec needed skilled laborers to replenish the workforce due in large part to Quebec's low birthrate. Around the same time, many Haitian intellectuals were seeking asylum from the Duvalier dictatorship. According to Guerda, the participant described above and one of the early Haitian migrants, this government-level desire to welcome laborers preceded wide acceptance of the idea of socially integrating foreigners at the level of the general population.

Quebec, a francophone nation within a larger anglophone nation, has fought to maintain French-Canadian ethnic and cultural identity, leaving many unsettled by the sudden influx of foreigners, even those who may be speakers of French. This feeling of viewing immigrants as forever foreign permeates a statement by Guerda. She told me about her entry into Quebec's workforce: "I remember when I was studying to become a nurse, an instructor told me that I was a representative of my country. And I thought, 'A representative of my country? What does that mean? I can't represent my country. I am from Haiti, but I'm not here to represent my country. No one gave me an ambassador's mandate. Would you evaluate me for who I am inside this course?'" Though Guerda did not think her nation of origin was particularly relevant in this setting where she was training for a professional career in Quebec, her race and ethnicity were at the forefront of her instructor's mind. As the earlier quote from Guerda about entering a new workplace demonstrates, her identity as a Black, Haitian woman continued to define her professional experiences in her interactions with colleagues. She was not welcomed and included in the medical team as a nurse; instead, she received the cold shoulder and was treated with suspicion as a foreign, Black nurse.

The wariness about foreigners in Montreal was largely expressed through anxieties about maintaining French-Canadian ethnic identity and a persistent assumption that Quebec's history is that of white French Canadians, despite the fact that today one in five people in Montreal are foreign-born. This racist xenophobia shapes the contours of cultural citizenship in Montreal, presenting an obstacle to Haitians and other minority groups to gaining full cultural citizenship.

In contrast to the general social unease reported by early migrants in Montreal, early Haitian migrants in Boston were met with overt racial slurs and threats to personal safety. This intense reaction stems from the particulars of the relationship between the United States, slavery, and the long and drawn-out process of desegregation. Haitians in Boston met racism from white Bostonians not for being "outsiders," but for being "Black," though Blackness and outsider status cannot be fully disentangled, since those processes of discrimination occur in concert. Haitian women sit at the intersection of anti-Black racism and xenophobia.

In Boston, African Americans were often considered outsiders, though not foreigners in the national context. At times, African Americans dissociated from Haitian migrants, perhaps in part because of the ways in which Haitian labor became more highly valued than African American labor. This labor hierarchy reinforced ethnic divisions between Haitians and African Americans but did not necessarily shield Haitians from the brunt of the racism directed toward Blacks regardless of their ethnicity. Though Haitians often began their working lives in Boston at the bottom of the labor hierarchy like Haitians in other places such as Miami, Haitians in Boston had a class advantage in Haitian society, and the transnational resources such as education and social networks that come with that class advantage, allowing them more social mobility than lower-class and poor Haitian migrants in the United States.

Josephine and her family moved to Boston in 1975 when she was in early adolescence. She told me that her life in Haiti before moving to the United States was uneventful. Her father owned a business, her family owned a home and had servants, and she and her siblings attended private schools. She does not know too much about her mother's decision to move to the United States, but it happened after her parents separated in Haiti. Josephine remembers feeling very scared when she first moved to Boston because some neighborhoods were unsafe and racism was extremely prevalent. In Haiti, she had someone to take her to and from school, comb her hair, and cook her food. Figuring out how to navigate Boston, including taking public transportation to school on her own when she did not yet speak English, was a shocking change for her. She knew that the move was permanent because her mother sold all their furniture before moving to the United States, but she still held onto the fantasy that she could return to that familiar life in Haiti one day. She describes her experiences in public school when she arrived in Boston as "traumatizing." Her family fell on hard times in Boston and her mother returned to Haiti, leaving Josephine and her siblings in Boston on their own. She was able to find employment through her school's work-study program. Josephine reflected on the racial and ethnic tensions in the city when she arrived:

There were certain areas in Boston you couldn't venture into because it could really cost—you could end up being very hurt. So, it was hard. I mean, I remember it being very scary, more scary than anything else. Because I lived in fear all the time, not knowing, not understanding. . . .

My sister probably had it a little easier than I did, but I went to [public high school]. At the time, it was being desegregated, and it was during busing. We were bused to school, with police escort. We had riots every other day. You're in class one minute, next thing you know, riot, boom, you're home. So, you were not getting a proper education. . . .

But you get thrust into Boston in the middle of desegregation and it's racist and it's cold. The Black kids don't like you. The white kids don't like you. The Haitian kids who are somewhat hip don't want to associate with you because you've just come.

Many immigrants know of racial tensions in the United States before migrating and are prepared to encounter a certain amount of structural racism, but sometimes they feel unprepared to face the interpersonal racism that they experience. While Haitians immigrating to the United States may not feel antagonism toward white Americans, since they did not historically experience slavery in the United States, white Americans often see Haitians as African American, and therefore may subject Haitians to the same racist treatment doled out to African Americans. This was particularly true for the early wave of immigrants in the 1960s and 1970s, many of whom had light skin and enjoyed a privileged status in Haiti prior to migrating.[6] The experience of racism may have been particularly shocking for the first major wave of Haitian immigrants in the 1960s, since they arrived in the United States amid racial tensions surrounding the civil rights movement. As Josephine noted, in Boston, many first-wave migrants found themselves in the middle of race riots over busing to desegregate schools.[7] Haitian immigrants have at times aligned themselves with African Americans and at other times defined themselves as distinctly separate from African Americans.[8] Contrary to descriptions of social unease experienced by Haitians in Montreal as connected to their status as foreigners, early Haitian migrants to Boston describe scenes of blatant racial hostility and violence directed at them because of their perceived similarities to African Americans. They found themselves caught between white (many Irish and Italian) and African American Bostonians.

Unlike in Montreal, many of the whites in Boston during the first wave of Haitian migration were descendants of relatively recent immigrants from Ireland and Italy themselves. Irish and Italian immigrants in the United States were at times racialized as less than fully white and struggled to negotiate their place in the racially and ethnically stratified paid labor market.[9] Attempting to maintain their ethnic identities from outsiders, white ethnic groups in Boston were largely outsiders themselves struggling to make a place in the existing racial hierarchies in the United States.

In both the Boston and Montreal contexts, the first wave of Haitian migrants in the 1960s and 1970s entered into contested and emergent racial hierarchies. The nuances of those hierarchies and the ways in which racial and ethnic identity are inflected varies depending on historical context of each site. These examples illustrate how racial tensions affected early Haitian migrants in work, in school, and in the streets. These racial hierarchies are central to the construction of cultural citizenship and determining who fully belongs in the nation.

In France, a purportedly universalist nation in which the state actively aims to erase racial difference, racism nonetheless persists but takes on different forms due to the taboo associated with the term "race." For this reason, racism in France often manifests in coded language about religion or culture. As the vast majority of Haitians are Christian, this religious alignment eases Haitian integration into French society in a way that Muslim immigrants from North Africa do not experience. Though secular in name, France's national work holidays reflect the Christian calendar, allowing Haitian migrants to integrate into the workplace more easily than immigrants of other faiths. As they were placed in relation with African Americans in Boston during the 1960s and 1970s, Haitians in Paris are situated above North African immigrants in France's social and economic hierarchies. The first major wave of emigration from Haiti occurred on the tails of Algeria's war for independence from France, a time when France as a nation was going through a crisis of identity as a colonial power.

The following section focuses on the nexus of race, ethnicity, and work to highlight the ways in which the workplace served as a stage upon which anxieties over race and ethnicity played out for Haitian workers and their colleagues, work being an important site where cultural citizenship is forged.

Working through Race and Ethnicity

Patrice, a quiet, older Haitian woman with dark brown skin, moved to the United States when she was thirty years old. In Haiti prior to moving, she worked as a secretary at a store in what she described as a "good job." Patrice decided to leave Haiti because the economic and political situation was unbearable and all her siblings already lived in the United States, though scattered between Boston, New York, and Chicago. She initially moved to Washington, D.C., to work as a nanny for a French family who wanted someone francophone to care for their children. Patrice was the youngest in her family, and her older sisters made the arrangements for her to take this job and immigrate to the States. Patrice did not like the job once she arrived, because it afforded her very little freedom and she was confined to taking care of the children in the home where she worked. Even though she described the economic and political situation in Haiti as unbearable, it was not so bad compared with her experience working as a nanny in D.C. Patrice described feeling "like a slave" working for that French family, having left the freedom and employment that she had previously enjoyed in Haiti. She stayed in the position for a year because she was under contract, but then she moved to Boston to join one of her sisters.

After moving to Boston, Patrice worked for a hotel chain where she became a supervisor. She much preferred this new employment and her supervisory role to her previous job taking care of children in the home. She would sometimes travel for work and teach new employees how to open new hotels. Patrice got married, and when she became pregnant with her son, she left the job at the hotel and undertook training to become a medical secretary instead. As part of the training program, they placed her in a job where she worked for thirty-one years. She loved the job so much she exclaimed, "God made that job for me!" In her current position, Patrice works as an interpreter for Haitian immigrants. She helps to connect Haitian patients with resources within the health care system and travels to homeless shelters to enroll people in Medicaid and Massachusetts state health care.

All of Patrice's work experiences in the United States were shaped by her race, gender, and nation of origin. As she was a Haitian immigrant, the first employment she was able to secure in the United States, allowing her to migrate, was working as a nanny, a low-wage and particularly racialized and gendered form of work. In her low-status work as a nanny, Patrice found paid labor to be extremely oppressive. She felt trapped in that employment and as though she had given up her freedom. As a Haitian woman, she was tracked into low-status work like so many other women of color. This social isolation in low-status work prevented Patrice from feeling that she had access to cultural citizenship. Patrice felt a sense of value and importance through her later jobs and regained a level of autonomy that had been stripped from her in the nanny position. Her life experience as a Haitian woman leaves her especially well-suited to help other immigrants in her current position. She not only achieved a level of cultural citizenship for herself through her labor but also worked to help other immigrants to attain cultural citizenship within the nation as well.

For Haitian women, the things that they share with middle-class white women in the United States because of gender are inflected differently because of race, citizenship status, and language, as well as gender.[10] S. Charusheela argues that paid work historically has had very different meanings for descendants of slaves and immigrants who are brought to metropoles to perform cheap labor. Charusheela goes so far as to assert, "The actual experience of work, far from being liberation from the bonds of home, was and is often demeaning, undignified, and oppressive."[11] In addition to the challenges of reframing normative gender relations within the household, women of color have experienced work outside the household as degrading but necessary for survival. Patrice described her experience working as a nanny for a family in Washington, D.C., as oppressive in a way that resonates with the literature about work for Black women. Patrice goes so far as to use the racially coded language of feeling "like a slave" to describe her early work in the United States. However, Patrice describes her later work experience in the health care system in Boston as being extremely fulfilling. (The theme of paid work as oppressive or emancipatory for Haitian women in diaspora will be further examined in chapter 4).

Flore, a thin and graceful light-skinned Haitian woman in her eighties, migrated to Boston during the late 1950s with her husband as one of the first Haitian families in Boston. Flore attended a Catholic school while growing up in Haiti and began working as a secretary when she was eighteen years old. Her father was the director of a big company, and she was able to find employment typing as a secretary there. She then stopped working when she married at age twenty-two and soon after had her first child. Flore's husband moved to Quebec initially to pursue his education and look for work because it was difficult finding work in Haiti, leaving her and their two young children in Haiti and sending for them to join him after he settled in Boston a year later. Flore did not know anyone besides her husband when she first moved to Boston, and she reports that they were one of only a handful of Haitian families in the area at the time.

Flore and her husband ultimately had five children, and in the early years in Boston, Flore stayed home to take care of them rather than working outside the home. She struggled with social isolation, in part because she did not speak English and in part because she was always home with the children. She missed her family who had stayed behind in Haiti and she descended into a depression. She used to cry, especially in the cold, dark winter months, but she always tried to put on a brave face for her children. When her youngest started school, Flore began to work for the public school system part-time as a lunch monitor.

Flore reflected on the influx of Haitians during the first major wave of migration in the 1960s and how American perceptions of Haitians shifted during that time period. During an interview in her home in a well-to-do suburb of Boston, with her daughter and grandchildren gathered in the next room, Flore told me,

> Because Haitian people, there is something good in Haitians. When they come here, they work. They see Haitian people will have two, three jobs. When they go to do a job, they work.
>
> Every Haitian who goes to the hospital, they like them because they're very hard workers. I don't know if you've heard that talk. But they are hard workers. They did like Haitians. Matter of fact, if you say you're Black, they say, "You're not Black, you're Haitian." But I don't know, you're not Black, you're Haitian. That's the way they used to put Haitian people. "You are not Black."
>
> That's the truth. And all of these people nearly come and they find jobs right away. There are a lot of them in hospital now. Because they are good workers, are real, real good workers. So that's again—see, some people, they have two, three jobs. They go to this hospital, they go and they go and do this. They're very good workers.

Perceptions that Haitians are hard workers and good employees, both from within immigrant communities and from dominant Western society, has led employers in North America and France to seek out Haitian women, often as domestic workers.[12] According to scholar Marilynn S. Johnson, some members of established ethnic groups in Boston valued what they perceived as the hard-work ethic of more recent immigrants, which they pitted in contrast to stereotypes of African Americans as lazy and poor.[13] Some newer immigrants chose to lean into this stereotype of them as hardworking in an attempt to side-step difficult racial conflict existing in their new homes.

Adding to the complexities in the relationship between native-born Blacks and Black immigrants, Johnson's statement about older white ethnic groups pathologizing native-born Blacks speaks directly to Flore's statement about Haitians being "good" and "hard workers" with the implication being that native-born Blacks are not "good" and not "hard workers." Whether or not Flore understood the work that her rhetoric was doing, the outcome of differentiating Haitians as separate from and better than native-born Blacks remains. In Boston's paid labor hierarchy, early Haitian migrants were clearly differentiated from African Americans. Almost every Haitian woman with whom I spoke in the older generation in Boston referenced the fact that employers believe Haitians to be good workers, often citing this stereotype with pride.

Further complicating this differentiation between Black immigrants and native-born Blacks, Mary C. Waters writes, "This cultural stereotype of black immigrants as more successful than native-born black Americans is deeply ingrained in American society."[14] In a study of African American and West Indian workers and their white managers in a corporate cafeteria in New York, Waters finds that structural reasons, such as hiring networks and hiring discrimination, lead uneducated migrants from the Caribbean to outperform African Americans of the same level of skill and education. Even though the difference in performance can be attributed to structural issues, white managers in this study use the gap in performance as reinforcement of stereotypes about African Americans.[15]

Many Haitian immigrants, particularly in the United States, are aware of this stereotype and consciously choose to embrace it, expressing great pride in the highly touted West Indian work ethic. This stereotype at times offers a strategically beneficial trope for Haitians to employ, allowing them entry into the paid workforce; however, the image of Haitians as efficient and productive employees continues to situate Haitian migrants as subservient to white Westerners and makes them targets for labor exploitation because of the assumption they will not or cannot complain.

The benevolent racism of categorizing Haitians as "good workers" conceals the historical and contemporary destabilization of the Haitian economy and exploitation of Haitian labor that has led so many Haitians to seek work abroad. Western nations have played a crucial role, though to varying degrees, in destabilizing Haiti economically, creating the conditions that require Haitians to seek employment through foreign companies or abroad. Dubbing Haitians as "good workers" sets them in conflict with other marginalized groups in search of work within gendered and racialized labor hierarchies and creates the image of Haitians as good lower-level employees who can follow orders, rather than as workers who occupy leadership roles.

Differentiating Haitians from African Americans as Flore's employers insisted sheds light on the racial tensions between white and African Americans at this time. White employers in certain circumstances privileged Haitian workers over African Americans, using the trope of Haitians as hardworking to situate Haitians above African Americans in the labor hierarchy. By privileging Haitians above African Americans, white employers fostered divisiveness along ethnic lines rather than a Black solidarity between African Americans and immigrants that could have had more power to challenge conditions in the workplace.

In stark contrast, Haitians I have spoken to in Montreal were surprised to hear of the prevalence of the "good worker" stereotype in Boston. Many in Montreal cite having been able to find fulfilling work despite the challenges of being Black immigrant women. Without the challenge of situating themselves in relation to the largely invisible native Black Quebecers, Haitians in Montreal cited their status as foreigners as more of a roadblock than the fact that they are Black. In Montreal, racism and xenophobia are inextricably linked, as someone who is Black is automatically assumed to be non-native.

For Haitians in Montreal, the race issues are more subtle than in the United States, often involving othering comments about hair or asking Haitian women to perform their Haitianness in some way in an overzealous, and sometimes offensive, display of multicultural appreciation. For instance, several Haitians in Montreal stated that coworkers would make offhand comments about their food in a sometimes complimentary but always othering manner.

Farah, who worked part-time as an event coordinator and part-time as a fitness coach, reported subtle forms of racism in Montreal. During an interview in a small, unfinished room at the center where she works as a fitness coach, Farah said,

> [Racism is] subtle here. It's very subtle. Sometimes if you don't have two situations you won't feel it. They hide it very well, but it's mostly in the job I have right now, because in the job I have I'm a receptionist and event coordinator. And then sometimes for example if I am at the reception desk, some people might come and they don't say "Hi." But I will notice that sometimes when I have a lot of work, I have a temp come to work as a second receptionist for four hours. Often she's blonde, someone white. If, for example, I am behind her, the same person who never says hello to me will greet her with, "Hi, how are you?" But with me they never say "Hello." So, it's like that, really subtle.
>
> But you really have . . . I'm not looking for racism, but there is a difference in comportment when there's someone who's like them, who's not me. For example, the Black employees in the office, and we don't have many, but there are two Black people out of eighty employees. There are differences. The white people, when they are together they are friends with each other, they walk together, they are always together, but the Black people have to walk alone and don't really have friends here.
>
> Here it's very subtle. If you don't find yourself in certain situations you would say, "Oh, it's a welcoming country, they love Black people, they love immigrants!" You know, if I'm in the States I know they don't like Black people so I will be careful, you know? But here, you tend not to be careful, but they are after you. They are really racist here but they hide it really well so you cannot say they are racist.

Farah describes the subtle forms of racism she encounters in the workplace in Montreal, and without prompting differentiates it from the type of racism she knows about in the United States. The United States often became the reference point for Haitian women in Montreal and Paris when discussing race. I suspect that was in large part because they were speaking with me, a Black American woman, but also because the United States has so much media attention and identifiable social movements associated with anti-Black racism.

U.S.-based theories of race and ethnicity can be used to inform transnational analyses, but only if thoughtfully applied with attention to how the local context shaped the development of those theories. I draw from the seminal works of renowned American feminist scholar Rose Brewer to examine how the lived experiences of Haitian women in diaspora might enable us to extend and augment current scholarship about how labor affects the lives of women of color in intersecting and historically constituted ways. The racial and gendered division of labor is rooted in social, and arguably cultural, systems of meaning.[16]

Looking particularly at the U.S. context, Brewer identifies the ways in which the position of Black women within the U.S. labor system reflects the historical and systematic oppression of Black women. Evelyn Nakano Glenn, also focusing on the United States, examines the intersection of race and labor in three local sites, creating a comparative historical analysis of race and gender, labor, and citizenship during the era of U.S. Reconstruction. While these two authors specifically write about the United States, I argue that their theories of race, gender, and labor as rooted in a cultural system of meaning and material relations can elucidate the racialized processes of citizenship-making in other nations as well, especially in this age of transnational neoliberalism. Simultaneously, the experiences of Haitian women in diaspora in this study can draw attention to how we need to adapt these theories when examining these processes outside of the United States.

Farah's experiences working in Montreal as a Black woman reflect the particular cultural and historical context of French Canadians attempting to guard themselves against any outside influence. Her experience of belonging in Montreal is shaped by ideas about who is truly Quebecois (white, French Canadians). Those ideas about citizenship and belonging play out in their workplace interactions, where her white colleagues subtly but clearly indicate to her that she does not belong there. Once again, cultural citizenship is formed along racial lines in the workplace.

Paris did not receive the same influx of Haitian migrants as did Montreal and Boston during the first wave of Haitian emigration under the Duvalier dictatorship; however, a small number of Haitians have lived, worked, and studied in France since the colonial days when Saint-Domingue was a French colony. In France, lack of a large, visible presence allows Haitians smoother integration than migrants from Africa and the Middle East. Similar to the ways in which Haitians situated themselves in relation to Black Americans in Boston, Haitians in Paris are situated in relation to Muslim, Black, and Arab North African immigrants. Though many North Africans are considered Arab rather than Black, the two categories are often collapsed to discuss "Otherness" and foreigners in France.

While the Haitian Revolution dealt a huge blow to France as an imperial power, the Algerian Revolution is a more recent military defeat that weighs heavily on French consciousness, particularly as large numbers of North Africans have migrated to France in recent decades. Many perceive the influx of North African migrants as a threat to the French nation, as it represents a reversal of the imperial flow of the French population which colonized North Africa. Though Haitians and North Africans are both racially non-white and therefore visually marked as not fully French, white Parisians consider Haitians to be closer to the ideal of "Frenchness" by way of their dress and affiliation with Christianity. In comparison to North Africans, Haitians are therefore considered more easily assimilated into the French nation. In the current moment where racism largely takes the shape of Islamophobia in France, eliding anti-Black racism under the umbrella of anti-Muslim sentiment, Christian Haitians are temporarily rendered part of the dominant French cultural identity that stands against immigrant and native-born French Muslims.

An example of this is the way that Mirlande, a middle-aged woman with light brown skin and one of my research participants in Paris in the summer of 2017, spoke about Muslims from North Africa. Each time I saw Mirlande she was dressed very modestly, in a matronly manner that makes her appear older than she is. Her hair is always pulled back into a tight bun at the nape of her neck, and she likes to wear colorful 1980s-style headbands. Mirlande first moved from Haiti to New York, and then from New York to Paris, where she lived, raised a family, and worked as a preschool teacher at a private school that did not require teachers to have a degree.

On several occasions, Mirlande made comments that signaled her dislike of North African Muslims. One day, we were leaving an event hosted by the Haitian Catholic Association in Paris. We left the church's reception area where the event was held and were walking side-by-side to the Metro. It was a Sunday afternoon, and there were hardly any other people on the sidewalk. Mirlande was telling me about how she brings books for the Haitian priest to read, and how she had just left him with a copy of Paulo Coelho's *The Alchemist*. Suddenly, Mirlande stopped her exuberant storytelling and fell silent. She then whispered under her breath with a hint of disdain, "I bet you don't see *that* in the United States." I saw a Black man walking toward us wearing traditional North African garb of a long tunic and a cap on his head. Pretending not to understand, I asked her to clarify. As we approached the man on the otherwise vacant, stone-paved sidewalk, Mirlande silently but emphatically gestured toward the man with her head and eyes.

On another occasion, Mirlande and I left a Haitian cultural event in another part of town in search of something to eat. It was after 3 P.M., and she complained that she hadn't eaten lunch because she had expected there to be food at the event. We asked for directions to the nearest restaurant and set off in the sweltering summer heat. We soon found a little pedestrian street scattered with small restaurants. The first place we came across advertised that they served Halal food. Mirlande quickly dismissed it as an option. Despite the fact that she was feeling faint with hunger, she told me that she would never trust "those people's" food.

Not all Haitian women in Paris expressed anti-Muslim sentiments like this, but Mirlande's case provides an extreme example of the ways in which Haitians are situated as separate from the Muslim, North African population of the city. In France, even French-born citizens of Algerian descent experience a disconnect between their place of birth and how they are perceived.[17] By way of religious affiliation and dress, Haitians find themselves more easily a part of the French population. In some cases that separation may be unintentional, though in Mirlande's case she very clearly and repeatedly differentiated herself from the North African Other. While differentiating herself from French Muslims, Mirlande still finds herself toward the bottom of the paid labor hierarchy, performing the racialized and gendered labor of caring for small children just like several other Haitian women I interviewed in Paris. Mirlande's Islamophobia makes her feel more French, but her integration into the French labor force doing gendered and racialized work betrays the limits of cultural citizenship.

At the core of Rose Brewer's analysis is the notion that women of color occupy a position within the paid workforce that is determined by race, gender, and class. Black women in the United States are often relegated to poorly paid, gender-segregated jobs, such as domestic labor and clerical work, and face disproportionate rates of unemployment while engaging in unpaid and devalued social reproductive labor.[18] Black women's placement within labor hierarchies in the United States remains intertwined with global neoliberal projects that systematically track women and minorities into insecure forms of employment, consisting of positions that fluctuate based on the ebbs and flow of capitalist market demands.[19]

Though Mirlande may feel a sense of superiority over Black Muslim immigrants in Paris, her positioning within the labor market reveals that her race and gender situate her toward the bottom of the paid labor hierarchy, just as Haitians in Boston. Though there are surely differences across context with regard to historical and contemporary constructions of race, global neoliberal projects connect the experiences of Black women across contexts in the way that Black women are consistently tracked into low-wage, low-status jobs.

By adapting Brewer's analysis of Black women's relationships to paid labor in the United States to look at experiences of Haitian women in Boston, Montreal, and Paris, I argue that the historical relationship of each nation to colonialism, racism, gender oppression, and xenophobia influences the ways that Haitian women become situated within the workforce. Similarly, I use a transnational analysis of the ways that Haitian women's labor connects them to forms of both membership and exclusion in various nations.

Mirlande and the several other Haitian women in Paris who work with young children experience inclusion in the nation through paid labor by having Christian holidays off and dressing in ways that are consistent with their French coworkers. However, they experience exclusion from the nation based on the kind of labor that is available to them as Black women and immigrants.

A handful of women across the sites worked for the United Nations (UN) or other large international organizations, both while in Haiti and while living abroad. Their language skills, often speaking French, Haitian Kreyòl, Spanish, and sometimes English, put them at an advantage in international agencies. The Haitian women who worked for the UN, however, spoke of a rigid hierarchy within the organization where Haitian women were often hired as local staff and white Americans and Europeans were frequently hired as international staff. Local staff are often paid less and of lower status than the international staff. Though language skills and cultural familiarity gained Haitian women entry into these large and powerful organizations, their positions within those organizations were frequently constrained by internal power dynamics that maintain hierarchies based on country of origin, and therefore race. Haitians are often put into "equity" positions where they are expected to liaise with the local population while having less room for growth and lower pay than white international staff.[20] These organizations are unique in that they foster an international consciousness in the workplace, cultivating a desire to travel and take part in multiple national contexts rather than remaining rooted firmly in a single country.

Tamara is a tall, middle-aged woman with very light skin dusted with freckles. When I interviewed her, she wore a long, gray dress that clung to her curves, and her short, straight, black hair was messily styled atop her head. Tamara participated in multiple national contexts from the time she lived in Haiti and worked first for the United Nations and then for the American Embassy. She came from a well-connected family in Haiti, and she knew the head of recruitment for the United Nations. After working for the United Nations, Tamara transitioned to a job with the American Embassy in Port-au-Prince.

Tamara enjoyed working for the American embassy. She said, "Oh, it's great. Americans are good with Haitians; they treat us well." She worked as an administrator and reported that the American consuls greatly appreciated her. Though Tamara had an enjoyable experience working for the American embassy, her work still situated her within racialized, global power dynamics. The presence of the American embassy speaks to the long relationship between the United States and Haiti, particularly during the U.S. occupation from 1915 to 1934, U.S. meddling in Haitian elections, and contemporary U.S. involvement in the form of coercive foreign aid.

Tamara needed to leave the American embassy for personal reasons and decided to move to Paris. Since she had previously worked for the United Nations in Haiti, it was relatively easy for her to transition into working for the organization again once she moved to France. While working for the United Nations Educational, Scientific, and Cultural Organization (UNESCO), an agency of the United Nations, in France, Tamara did a lot of work with African countries, especially Tanzania. After working for UNESCO, she went on UN Peacekeeping operations in Africa.

The United Nations was founded in the United States and largely maintains Western ideals across the globe. As a Black woman and a native of Haiti, Tamara was tracked into a particular career path within the United Nations that rendered her subordinate to her white American and European counterparts while in Haiti. She was able to negotiate her positioning within the United Nations from being local staff in Haiti to working as a Paris-based employee. As part of UNESCO and the UN Peacekeeping Operations, Tamara was situated in a position of power over the Africans with whom she interacted.

In addition to the experiences of Haitian women in these three nation-states, Haitians also participate in paid labor within international organizations such as the United Nations. While the United Nations does not represent any single nation, it broadly represents the interests of the West. Thus, the United Nations is a transnational organization with a disproportionately Western agenda. Within the United Nations, the organization creates structures and hierarchies that continue to privilege employees from North American and Western European nations and track employees from Haiti into subordinate administrative roles. In this way, global racial and ethnic hierarchies are reinforced through employment within the United Nations; however, at moments, Haitian women are able to negotiate their positioning within the United Nations. In one example, a Haitian woman moved to Montreal before working for the United Nations in a supervisory capacity over staff in Barbados. In another example, Tamara moved to Paris and then traveled to work in Africa as a representative of France.

Race, work, and belonging function similarly within the United Nations as within workplaces that are grounded within a singular national context, only with the United Nations, Haitian women achieve belonging in a powerful transnational network through their paid labor rather than belonging within a nation. Though the United Nations is a transnational organization, the same rules of global capital and stratified labor based on race and gender still apply. Race, gender, and nation of origin continue to shape Haitian women's relationship to power in the United Nations, just as in other workplaces in Boston, Montreal, and Paris. While I argue that paid labor is a crucial site where cultural citizenship is negotiated within national contexts, within the United Nations, paid labor is a site where global citizenship is negotiated and global racial and ethnic hierarchies are reinforced.

Applying Black Feminist Theory Transnationally

I met Naomi at an event hosted by Maison d'Haïti, the major Haitian cultural center in Montreal. She spoke on a panel featuring scholars and activists involved in the Haitian community. I introduced myself after the panel, and we stayed in contact during my time in Montreal and beyond. She is a doctoral student in her mid-thirties with very light skin and curly hair. Naomi was born in Haiti and lived her early years in her family home in Pétion-ville, an affluent suburb of Port-au-Prince. She remembers her childhood home as lush and beautiful, as her mother loved gardening. Naomi migrated with her family first to Europe and then to Quebec City when she was young. She has lived in Montreal since she was a teenager and got her first job there as a community organizer. She started out volunteering for a community organization in Little Burgundy, a working-class neighborhood of Montreal that is home to a Black anglophone population, Irish immigrants, and more recently, immigrants from the Caribbean as well. As she was volunteering for this community organization, they started to secure grants to pay her so that her volunteering turned into her first paid employment. Following high school, Naomi returned to Haiti to work at a school with her aunt in Jérémie, a city in the south of the country. Naomi described this time as an attempt to make peace with Haiti, the country she left as a young girl but to which she held on to hope that she would return. She is extremely well-connected in various communities in Montreal and always involved with activism alongside her doctoral studies.

On a cold night in January of 2017, Naomi and I met up for an interview over hot chocolate in a café in Montreal. In addition to the formal interview, we talked for hours about our lives and our research. That evening Naomi told me, "It's hard because I don't really identify with U.S. Black feminist [theory], though I have a lot of respect for it and understand the context in which it arose."

This quote led me to ask the question of what is missing for Naomi when she looks at U.S. Black feminist theory. I posit that what is missing for her is an acknowledgment of how U.S.-based theories fit within a transnational racial framework. Her comment emphasizes how race and ethnicity cannot be fully understood without historical and cultural context. Much of the rich literature on race and ethnicity in U.S. sociology has focused specifically on race within the context of the United States. To explore race transnationally, scholars must be careful not to apply uncritically U.S.-based theories and concepts to other contexts, and to remain mindful of the contexts within which theories are developed. I hope that this chapter applies Brewer's work in a way that respects the unique histories and specificities of each site, rather than blindly applying

American scholarship in an act of intellectual imperialism. In addition to the wealth of scholarship produced on race and ethnicity in the U.S. context, we can also draw from the work of postcolonial scholars such as Frantz Fanon, Paul Gilroy, Stuart Hall, Jacqui Alexander, and others.[21] Though the work of postcolonial scholars such as these provides one piece of the puzzle for analyzing race transnationally, the focus of this chapter is the ways in which U.S.-based scholarship on race can be used with care to study race transnationally. Through transnational analyses of the ways in which race and ethnicity are constructed, we can build upon existing theories, testing, challenging, and developing ever-more-nuanced understandings of race and ethnicity. Yet I contend that aspects of U.S. Black feminist theory can do important work in describing and analyzing how the worksite becomes a place of racial formation.

Conclusion

Race and ethnicity exist across national borders, but the local context always inflects the ways in which these categories manifest and shape people's daily lives. This transnational examination of work, race, and ethnicity illustrates the ways in which race and ethnicity are constructed and contested across different spaces. Racism exists in each of these locations in some form, but the way that it manifests is strictly related to the specific history of each locale. We can talk about concepts of race and ethnicity transnationally, but only while remaining grounded in the specificities of individual locations. Scholarship on race that has been developed based solely on the U.S. context, such as the work of Rose Brewer, can help to reveal processes of race and ethnicity in other places. However, we must be cautious and deliberate when applying U.S.-based race theories to other contexts, for blindly applying U.S. theories of race to the rest of the world is an act of scholarly imperialism and misses the nuances of space, place, and history.

The experiences of these Haitian women demonstrate that racism manifests differently across location, and that the particular expression of racism is dependent on each location's historical context. Race is a concept that transcends national boundaries, but it is complex and constantly shifting in its manifestations. The way we see race in daily workplace interactions for Haitians in Boston differs from the way that race and racism play out in Montreal or Paris. Manifestations of racial difference also shift across time, though the historical context informs contemporary expressions of race and racism. For instance, Haitian migrants during the 1960s and 1970s faced different social and political climates than those who emigrated in more recent years; that said, the history of race riots in Boston during the 1970s and the push for multicultural inclusion continue to inform the city's current racial climate.

This chapter examined the ways in which positioning within the paid labor system, in both national and international contexts, shapes the manifestations of race and ethnicity for Haitian women in diaspora. The above examples include instances where Haitian women in Boston, Montreal, Paris, and the United Nations experienced and took part in shaping racial formations inside and outside the workplace. Both the movement of Haitian women transnationally and the presence of international organizations draw attention to the ways in which race and ethnicity exist not only within discrete locales but between and among locales. Using the method of multisited ethnography, the experiences of Haitian women in this chapter highlight the interconnectedness of place and nations when examined through the lens of race and paid labor. The interconnectedness of race and ethnicity across sites is precisely what enables us to adapt the work of U.S. feminist scholars on race and labor to help explain the relationship between race and paid labor transnationally as well.

4

Gender Roles and Work, In and Out of the Home

Even in your country, you have servant, you have people, maid to serve you, and you come here, you're a maid serving people, and those people didn't even show appreciation.
—Patrice, Boston

I argue in this chapter that gender and class shape the opportunities and experiences of work for Haitian women and that gendered expectations with regard to work are reconstituted post-migration. I also assert that paid labor provides agency and independence to Haitian women while simultaneously perpetuating their subordinate status with regard to gender and class. I will examine the experiences of Haitian women and work through the lens of gender, highlighting how gender roles shift upon migration with regard to work, how Haitian women are often tracked into low-status, low-wage gendered labor, and how even low-status work can serve as a source of pride and independence while simultaneously reinforcing the subordination of Black, immigrant women within the paid labor hierarchy. In addition, I will also analyze how class intersects with expectations surrounding gender and work for Haitian women as they undergo a decline of class status through the process of migrating from Haiti, a globally marginalized country with limited economic and political influence on the global stage, to the United States, Canada, and France, all global superpowers.

This chapter builds on the work of scholars of gender and labor, such as Rose Brewer and S. Charusheela, as well as scholars who seek to illuminate the relationship between gender and migration, including Patricia Pessar and Sarah Mahler, extending literature on gender, work, and migration.[1] I examine how Haitian women in diaspora experience work in ways that reveal how work, both unpaid domestic labor and paid labor outside of the home, is classed and gendered, situating women's work within the raced, classed, and gendered hierarchies of the nation.

Just as chapter 3 demonstrated how race is constituted and reaffirmed through work, in this chapter I illustrate the deep connections between gender and labor in the lives of Haitian migrants, pointing to how one's relationship to paid and domestic labor shapes the expression of one's gender roles, and how simultaneously one's gender shapes one's relationship to labor. For the Haitian women in this study, their gender roles were strongly shaped by their class status.

Gendered labor exists in each of the locations in this study not because these three locales are unique; rather, the presence of gendered labor across these locales indicates that the process of gendering certain labor as undervalued women's work takes place across and between locales. The Haitian women in this study employed other women to perform that gendered labor before migrating. After migration, they found themselves engaging in gendered labor, both within their homes and oftentimes in their paid work outside the home. Cultural citizenship for these women includes adopting some of the gender practices of their new national context but also maintaining other gender practices from their nation of origin.

Although I draw from women's experiences in Canada and France, in this chapter I focus heavily on the stories of women in Boston, as the themes surrounding gender and class stood out most strikingly in conversations with Haitian women in the Boston area. Focusing heavily on the Boston context while examining this theme allows us to see clearly how gender is constituted and negotiated through labor. Though focused on a particular subsection of the population, I connect the lived experiences of Haitian women in diaspora with broader themes of race, gender, and labor.

To begin, Roseline, a woman in Boston in her early sixties with short, natural hair and a very funny and relaxed demeanor, described a shift in her class awareness upon moving to the United States. Roseline's mother moved to Boston first. Her mother was the director of an orphanage in Port-au-Prince but was not paid consistently and needed to work as a seamstress making dresses for upper-class women to make ends meet. Roseline's family was not wealthy, but Roseline attended a private school with students from the upper class. When Roseline's mother learned of an opportunity through a friend in Port-au-Prince to move to Boston to work as a maid for a wealthy family, she decided to make the move for economic reasons. This was in the 1970s, and though she did not know anyone in Boston prior to moving, she had other friends in Haiti who were taking similar opportunities at the same time. Like many other Haitian women who moved to Boston during that first wave of migration, Roseline's mother was able to immigrate because of her raced, classed, and gendered positioning within the global labor hierarchy. Around that time, job opportunities to work as maids, a distinctly gendered type of labor, enabled many Haitian women to obtain green cards to move to the United States.

Roseline's mother moved to Boston when Roseline was seventeen or eighteen; Roseline stayed in Port-au-Prince with her godmother for a year to finish high school before joining her mother. While sitting across a small table from me in a café down the street from her office in downtown Boston, Roseline explained:

> Coming here, though, I had certain expectations. I remember my mother sent me five dollars and I thought, she makes eighty dollars a week and she only sends me five dollars a month! And of course, she would send more money to my godmother to take care of me, but for me it was only five dollars and I was very disappointed. So, I come here and I think I'm going to be rich. So, I go to my first job and that was also . . . I mean I had five years of English and I had good grammar and vocabulary, but I couldn't pronounce words correctly.
>
> And in Haiti, because we're a poor country, we have maids. People were addressing me the way that I would address the maids in Haiti, which also made me empathize to the way I was treating the maids because you just assumed they have nothing going on there. And you know, they would talk to you like you were stupid, like, please repeat what I said to make sure you understand, and these were things I would do to the maids, like when I would give them instructions and I would ask them to repeat it back. But it never occurred to me that that was . . . when you're on the receiving end of it it's not very nice. So, it was mixed.

After she began working in the United States, Roseline realized that she was suddenly treated the way that she used to treat the maids in Haiti. In Haiti, she did not have to work while finishing high school and she was accustomed to having lower-class women take care of her basic needs in the household. Once she began working, she realized that she was now the lower-class working woman on whom others looked down as inferior or simple-minded. Not only did Roseline now need to take care of her own domestic labor, but she was also newly in the position of performing gendered, caring labor for others. In this way Roseline reflects on her new position as marginalized in the United States, as well as her previous class position in Haiti.

Alongside shifts in gender roles, migration for Haitian women also involves a shift in class status that influences the ways in which gender roles become expressed through labor. I look at the roles of both paid labor and unpaid domestic labor in shaping the way that Haitian women in diaspora experience gender and class. By troubling categories of "gender" and "class" through their relationships to labor, Haitian women reveal how these categories are malleable and shaped by local context. These at times taken-for-granted categories are continually shifting and constituted.

Haitian women in Boston, Montreal, and Paris reported numerous problems associated with paid labor, including everything from sexual harassment in the workplace to husbands forbidding them from returning to work after marriage or childbirth. On top of the challenges of paid work, rather than freeing women of color from the bonds of the household, work outside the home involves a double day for many women, as they must perform work outside the home while also taking care of their families. Despite the trials associated with engaging in paid labor and taking on domestic labor, often for the first time, many Haitian women expressed great pride in their work. Work played a multifaceted role in the lives of these women, sometimes leading to the reorganization of traditional gender roles in the home and at other times reinforcing existing gender roles through gendered labor.

Alongside changing gender roles, Haitian migrant women typically experienced an abrupt change in class status. This shift in class status at times necessitated the evolution of traditional gender roles to maintain a household without the help of household staff. The flexibility of prescribed gender roles in relation to domestic and other labor illuminates the ways in which gender roles are constructed in a particular place and time and can shift based on circumstances. Women engage in gendered work in each location, and participants in this study demonstrate that at least in Boston and Montreal, Haitian women have at times negotiated domestic labor arrangements with their male partners. This does not mean that similar negotiations did not take place in Paris, only that the sample size (and target population) was too small to uncover those experiences if they are present. The experiences of Haitian women in diaspora in this study signal to the strong connections between the construction of gender, class, and work, with implications for better understanding the interplay between these categories more broadly transnationally.

A New Relationship to Work

Many immigrants who were members of the middle and upper classes in Haiti experienced a downward shift in class status in their new host societies.[2] Along with this initial loss of class status upon migrating comes a new relationship to work, in terms of both paid labor outside the home and unpaid domestic labor. This was the case for many of the women with whom I spoke for this project.

In Haiti, only a few of the women performed housework. As members of the middle and upper classes, their families typically kept domestic servants to cook, clean, and raise children. This mirrors findings from Rhacel Salazar Parreñas's findings on Filipino domestic workers who, even as they worked in undervalued, low-status jobs in affluent Western countries, often employed women in more marginalized classes back home to perform domestic labor including caring for children and the elderly.[3] Maxine Margolis similarly notes what she describes as the transition "from mistress to servant" for Brazilian immigrants in New York City in which immigrants from the middle class in Brazil become confined in low-status work once arriving in the United States.[4]

The women I met throughout fieldwork also experienced a sudden class shift upon moving. This is a particularly gendered burden that disproportionately affects Haitian women, as gender norms from both Haiti and the host societies entail an expectation that women are predominantly responsible for child-rearing, cooking, and housekeeping.

Nadège, a tall, regal, light-skinned woman who migrated to Boston as a young, pregnant wife in 1968, explained: "Because I didn't know how to cook, you know? I didn't know nothing like to run a house. Because back there, you have people to do those things for you. So, I had to adjust and learn how to cook, you know, take care of kids, my new child, my husband, you know? Because those Haitian guys they don't do nothing! [laughter] The women have to do everything! So, it was a big change." Emphasizing the fact that there are differing expectations when it comes to domestic labor for Haitian men and Haitian women, Nadège's narrative reveals how in Haiti, working-class women were responsible for cooking, cleaning, and child-rearing, leaving middle-class women time for leisure and to pursue careers. Moving from Haiti to Boston, Nadège could no longer rely on the work of lower-class women to maintain her household, leaving her to take on the domestic labor that was previously delegated to women of a lower class. While Nadège and the other women in this study relied on the labor of lower-class women in Haiti, they then sometimes became the lower-class women who worked for others after migration. These women experienced class shifts within a global hierarchy where living a comfortable middle- or upper-class lifestyle in Haiti then translates to becoming a subordinate to whites abroad.

Not all women felt a seismic shift in their relationship to domestic labor upon leaving Haiti. Mona was an outlier in the group because of her attitudes toward work, migration, and belonging. In contrast to Nadège and Roseline, though her family had maids in Haiti, Mona, a woman in her fifties with dark skin and a medium build, expressed great pride in the fact that she used to help the maids with the housework. I spent time with Mona, her sister, and their elderly mother in their family home in Boston, a dark, three-story building in a lower-middle-class residential area. Mona emphatically relayed,

> Because you can't depend on anybody but yourself. So, if I still depend on the mentality that I was brought up, always thinking there would be somebody taking care of my business that I needed, someone to go get my shoes for me, I didn't go look for them if I didn't have to. My food was always on the table. I didn't have to wash dishes or anything like that, but as a young girl, I remember when I was in Haiti, I always participated in the housework. The maid in our home, to me, I didn't look at them as a maid, I look at them as part of the family. So, when they were cooking, I was there in the kitchen with them. If they were ironing, I was there helping them out, and say we would go upstairs and put somebody's clothes away or whatever. So, I think, that's what makes me who I am today.

Because of her experience helping the maids in in Haiti, Mona felt more pre-pared than other women in this study to step into the role of performing housework upon migrating to the United States. I want to emphasize again that Mona's experience of performing housework alongside the maids in Haiti as a member of the middle class was a highly uncommon experience for the women in this study. While sometimes referring to employees as "like family" makes invisible the work that is done or justifies exploitation, here Mona emphasizes working alongside her maids to help take care of the household in a very tan-gible way. I highlight Mona's experience because it indicates how her partici-pation in the housework as a child growing up in Haiti gave her the skills necessary to take care of herself without the help of maids once she lived in Bos-ton, easing at least that part of the transition.

Many Haitian women also experienced a profound shift when it comes to race or color as related to social class. Upon migration to the United States, Canada, and France, they found themselves at the bottom of the paid labor hierarchy as Black women. Haiti is a Black nation, but even within a Black nation there are issues of colorism. The middle and upper classes in Haiti are predominantly light skinned, while the poor and working classes are predom-inately dark skinned, a holdover from colonial times when white colonists and the mulatto elite maintained power over Black slaves.[5] Through migration, these Haitian women went from occupying a position of relative power and privilege as light-skinned women in Haiti to being near the bottom of the race hierarchy as Black women in the United States, Canada, and France.[6]

Finding Independence

One subtheme that seemed to appear only in the Boston examples is the idea that Haitian women may find paid work to be a source of independence. A factor that may contribute to the strong presence of this theme in Boston may be a partial adoption of the American Dream ideology, which holds that immigrants come to the United States to work for a better life and that through hard work they will achieve monetary success and full inclusion within American society. Though Haitian women in Montreal and Paris similarly engaged in paid labor, they did not talk about their work in the same way the women in Boston did. This finding is particularly notable when considering that Haitian women in Boston frequently started out working in low-status jobs such as cleaning or working in factories.

Another factor perhaps contributing to the overrepresentation of Haitian women in Boston in this chapter is that the vast majority of Haitians I interviewed in Boston migrated during the first major wave of immigration under Duvalier in the 1960s and 1970s. While some of the participants in this study in Montreal and Paris are of a similar age and migrated around the same time, in Montreal especially there were a number of younger Haitian women who migrated in the early 2000s. Expectations surrounding gender roles and work, both unpaid domestic labor and paid labor outside the home, have shifted over the years such that there is no longer an expectation that middle- and upper-class Haitian women will supervise the household and stay out of the paid workforce. A handful of Haitian women in Montreal whom I spent time with conducted their university studies and started careers while in Haiti prior to migrating. Their relationship to paid labor underwent a much less dramatic shift than the older generation of Haitian women in Boston who started careers from scratch in the United States. Many of the women who were credentialed professionals in Haiti, such as nurses and doctors, did not have their training and credentials recognized in their new homes abroad. Some chose to redo training to pursue their previous careers, but many ended up pursuing different career paths instead of starting over.

However, though the Haitian women who began their careers in Haiti prior to migrating to Montreal might not have experienced as sharp of a shift when it came to working outside the home in Montreal, they still experienced the challenges of domestic labor, including cooking, cleaning, and childcare, without the support of maids and nannies whom they had employed in Haiti. The theme of negotiating gender roles in the home came up in the experiences of almost every woman with whom I spoke for this book, from those who migrated during the first wave to those who migrated more recently in the 2000s.

The complicated relationship that Haitian women maintained with paid labor in Boston is reminiscent of the old feminist debate of whether paid labor is emancipatory or oppressive, perhaps especially for women of color. While many white U.S. feminists saw middle-class white women entering the paid workforce as a major step forward for women, Black feminist scholar Rose Brewer asserts that since the time of slavery, Black women in the United States have been exploited and oppressed through their labor.[7] In Boston, many of these women who were in the middle and upper classes prior to migration suddenly found themselves working for the first time. Though they describe the work as difficult, a number of these women also expressed great pride in their work and excitement over the opportunity to work and make money of their own. Even though the work itself may have been degrading, earning money offered them a sense of independence that many of them had previously not experienced.

Rather than neatly falling into the old debate over paid work being emancipatory or oppressive, the Haitian women in this study reveal complex relationships to paid labor. For many of these women, it was both, as it allowed them to provide for themselves rather than relying wholly on parents or husbands, but also meant they found themselves near the bottom of an established paid labor hierarchy as Black women. Perhaps more importantly, the Haitian women in this study illuminate how paid labor does more than emancipate or oppress them: it situates them within the nation in terms of their race, ethnicity, gender, and class. In this way, paid labor is a site where cultural citizenship is negotiated.

Rather than supporting this dichotomous oppressive versus emancipatory debate, the lived experiences of these women embrace both sides, suggesting that paid labor plays a more nuanced and critical role in the lives of Haitian women in diaspora.

These Haitian women's experiences illuminate how malleable gender roles can be and how gender roles are greatly dependent on class, location, relationship to the paid workforce, and the nation. While prior to migration many middle- and upper-class Haitian women, particularly those in the first wave of migration, did not work outside the home and instead oversaw lower-class women who performed domestic labor in their homes, after migration, out of necessity, most of those middle- and upper-class Haitian women began to engage in paid labor outside the home as well as unpaid domestic labor.

The experiences of Haitian women in this study also shed light on the relationship between class, gender, and paid labor for Haitian women but also how these forces play out for people transnationally depending on their intersectional positioning within raced, classed, and gendered global labor hierarchies. Haitian women in diaspora are caught up in global processes that shape their lives and opportunities. Those global processes affect us all, albeit in different ways depending on our relationships to power and privilege.

Gender Roles in the Home

The process of reconstituting gender relations for Haitian women post-migration to the United States, Canada, and France encompasses a similarly complex system of retaining certain aspects of gender norms while shifting and revising others. My analysis shows that the process is not uniform across all Haitian women who emigrate but that some circumstances facilitate a certain amount of flexibility when it comes to traditional gender norms for Haitian men and women.

In addition to developing a new relationship to work, Haitian women who emigrate to Boston, Montreal, and Paris also undergo a transformation in terms of their position within a racial hierarchy, which often plays out in gendered ways. For instance, many Haitian men of the same class did not perform domestic labor in Haiti and continued not to perform domestic labor after migrating, regardless of changes to race, color status, and class. That burden tends to fall heavily on Haitian women because of gender norms both in Haiti and in their host societies. As stated by Nadège, Haitian men do not traditionally partake in the domestic labor of cooking, cleaning, and raising children even after migration, leaving Haitian women to take on these household tasks often in addition to working outside the home.

Christine, a tall, dark-skinned woman with short hair who immigrated to the United States in the late 1960s as a young teenager with her grandmother and sisters, relayed that she experienced expectations not only about the role of women in the home but specifically about the role of Haitian women in the home. Christine originally moved to New York to reunite with her mother who had taken a job as a domestic worker at a family's home. Christine's mother originally found the job because she catered events for the American Embassy in Haiti and was able to make a connection through a friend to have her new employer in New York sponsor her visa. Once Christine and her sisters arrived in New York, they would go with people in their social networks to factories and other places of low-status employment to see if they could find work. Christine was young enough at the time that initially she only attended school, but one of her sisters had already completed high school in Haiti and immediately began working.

Christine later moved to Boston with her family, where she continued her schooling and found a job of her own to help pay for her high school tuition:

> I could have gone further if, I guess, if we had the help from the beginning. You know, because we practically had to try, we, on my own had to try to find help to pay for college. Even when I went to [Catholic high school], I had to help my mother pay for my tuition. So, you know? It's like, a lot of the time is spent

working, because, you know, I worked when I was in high school, instead of . . .
I don't know, going to a better school or things like that, but, you know . . .

Christine explained that assumptions about gender roles for Haitian women
followed her and shaped her relationship with her husband in her first
marriage:

> When I was married, even though I wasn't married to a Haitian, but that guy,
> he was like, he thinks that because I'm Haitian that's what you're supposed to
> do. "You're married to me, you're supposed to clean, you're supposed to wash
> my clothes and clean the house, and the kids and everything." That's exactly
> what you're supposed to do, with the kids, take them to babysit, pick them up,
> go to school, come here. Not only, that's, I guess, what the Haitian people think
> you have to do, but now that's the expectation, like, that other people's getting.

> NC: So about Haitian women? Not just about women in general but specifi-
> cally about Haitian women?
> C: Yeah. My experience, because I can tell you for sure, because my ex-husband,
> he knew. He'd say, "Oh yeah, that's why I want a Haitian woman, because I
> know my people won't do that; they won't."

For Christine, gendered expectations around domestic labor in the United
States compounded with expectations about Haitian women in particular. Her
African American ex-husband suggested that an American woman might not
be willing to take on all the domestic labor but that a Haitian woman would.
The intersecting oppressions of gender and nation of origin situated Christine
in an unequal power dynamic with her ex-husband where she felt trapped by
the gendered expectations of what it meant to be a Haitian woman in Boston.
In line with studies of whether gender roles from their country of origin persist for immigrants in Canada and the United States, Christine confirmed that
gender roles from Haiti continued to shape the division of labor in her marriage to her ex-husband; however, Christine's story complicates the findings of
those existing studies by suggesting that it is not only immigrants who bring
over and maintain gender norms but also Christine's U.S.-born ex-husband,
who maintained gender roles based on his assumption of what it means to be
a Haitian woman.[8]

Christine's experience of gender roles in the family as a Black immigrant
woman augments traditional ideas of gender roles in the home that are based
on white families. The "market-family matrix" is a framework by Dawn Marie
Dow that challenges prominent assumptions about the relationship between
dominant ideologies of the cult of domesticity and separate spheres that are frequently thought of in terms of white, middle-class women's experiences.[9] Dow

discusses the ideologies of the cult of domesticity and separate spheres: "These ideologies informed the dominant market-family matrix and dictated a specific gendered division of labor in the home and the workplace, whereby under "ideal" circumstances wives are principally responsible for duties within the family, yet defer to their husbands, and husbands are principally responsible for duties in the marketplace."[10]

Dow asserts that African American women and white women encounter different forces that shape their positioning in relation to the market-family matrix. Based on the experiences of Haitian women in this study, I extend Dow's analysis by contributing that even within race, Haitians and African Americans experience the market-family matrix differently based on their histories. While African American women in the United States have been integrated in the workforce since the time of slavery, many of the Haitian women in this study, particularly in the first wave of migration, were not expected to work outside the home as members of the middle and upper classes in Haiti. Though the cult of domesticity and separate spheres ideologies have been theorized within the context of the United States, Haitian women of the middle and upper classes have encountered similar ideological formulations with regard to expectations of ideal womanhood.[11] Upon migration to the United States, Canada, and France, most of these women engaged in paid labor outside the home alongside other racially and economically marginalized women in those countries.

Though the women in this study largely took on the burden of housework in addition to work outside the home during the class transition from Haiti to their host countries, there are some instances of shared housework between man and woman partners. For instance, Sandra moved to Montreal with her husband and their two-year-old daughter in 2007. In Haiti, her family was well-off and had maids and nannies to handle the housework and childcare, while Sandra and her husband pursued their careers. Upon moving to Montreal, however, their downward class mobility made it impossible for them to continue to hire domestic laborers as they had in Haiti. Sandra and her husband then found it necessary to take on domestic labor to support their growing family in addition to paid labor outside the home.

Sandra and her family lived on the first floor of a typically Verdun apartment, a brick, multifamily home in a residential area. Verdun is a historically working-class neighborhood of Montreal that was undergoing gentrification and did not house a substantial Haitian population. As I arrived, Sandra said that she was in the process of cleaning up and had almost finished. Sandra apologized for the mess and explained that she has three daughters, ages eleven, six, and two. She is a very small woman, both short and thin, with deep brown skin and black hair kept in shoulder-length locs. The apartment had very dark hardwood floors and felt a bit old, perhaps in need of renovations. Overall, the home was cluttered and well lived in. Upon entering, we passed a small, dark living room with a large, decorated Christmas tree that took up a huge portion of the room though it was late January. We continued back to the dining room and Sandra motioned for me to sit at the table. One end of the four-person rectangular table was covered in clutter, so I chose a seat by a clear spot on the table. I hesitated to put down my folder because there were little pieces of rice in front of me on the table. Sandra busied herself with tidying the table and wiped down the surface with a paper towel before sitting to join me. Sandra swiftly and seemingly unthinkingly took on the responsibility of cleaning up for me as a guest, a typically gendered role in the household.

For some, moving to a new country and undertaking paid labor outside the home necessitates creative reshuffling of traditional gender expectations when it comes to housework and child-rearing. Sandra and her husband disrupted traditionally gendered expectations of divisions of labor. Sandra explained:

> Since we moved here, my husband always works weekends. He always has jobs where he has to work weekends. So, his schedule now is that his weekends are Monday and Tuesday. So, I arrange my schedule so that I can work more those two days and some evenings when he's here. And he's not a typical Haitian man. He's the one who cooks for dinner; I do breakfast and dinner for the kids. He helps a lot; he does laundry. So, he helps a lot. He gets home from work around five, and he has time to take care of the kids.

Sandra homeschooled their children during the day while her husband was at work, and then her husband took over the childcare in the evenings and weekends. He also cooked and did laundry for the family, leaving Sandra time to attend to her entrepreneurial pursuits.

> Except, I'm not a full-time stay-at-home teaching mom because my life always has to be exciting! [laughter] I teach Zumba currently. I'm a Zumba teacher, and I started when I gave birth to my third one. A friend of mine was like, "Okay, let's be accountability partners so I can start my business." And I was like, "Okay," but then I realized it was so that *we* could start our separate businesses.
>
> . . .
>
> At some point I was like, maybe I can use all my psychology background plus my fitness background and combine that. So, I started being like a mind-body coach, but now I'm starting to become an eating psychology coach because I had an eating disorder when I was younger, so that's one of the reasons. So, last year I started being coached by a business coach and I started having clients. So, I do distance sessions over the phone or on Skype. I have

private clients. Last year I did workshops and I want to do more. I'm creating
my website, actually.

While in Haiti, Sandra and her husband were able to rely on the labor of lower-
class women to maintain the household and take care of their children while
they pursued their careers outside the home, but upon moving to Montreal,
instead of resorting to traditional prescriptions for gendered labor in the
household, Sandra and her husband found creative ways to arrange their sched-
ules so that they both engaged in caring labor in the home and pursued their
careers. Sandra's renegotiation of gender roles in the household resonates with
the "strident embedded agency" that Namita Manohar witnessed in middle-
class Tamil women migrants.[12] Similarly to the experiences of Haitian women
in diaspora exercising agency in (re)negotiating gender norms, Manohar notes
that the Tamil women's strident embedded agency is "gendered and grounded
in their transnational caste/class locations."[13]

One may think that Sandra's distribution of household labor speaks to the
time period and generation of which Sandra and her husband are a part;
however, similar to Sandra and her husband, Edwidge's Haitian parents challenged traditional Haitian and American gender roles of the household division of labor upon immigrating to Boston in the late 1960s. Edwidge, a sharp
and impeccably dressed professional woman in Boston with medium-brown
skin, is short in stature, but she was decked in tall, pointy heels and sported
perfectly coiffed, relaxed, dark-brown hair pulled back into a low bun. She
recounted the way that her parents balanced working outside the home and
maintaining the household upon migration: "My father was very supportive.
Because my father was working, I think he was working seven to three and my
mother worked later. And my father was always someone that—my father's
always a go-getter. When we would get home, he would start dinner. And he
still cooks. He would start dinner and my mother would finish it." Even as part
of the first major wave of emigration, Edwidge's parents shared at least some of
the housework that was frequently viewed as a woman's domain in both Haitian and American cultures. It is important to note that the reshuffling of gender roles in the household demonstrated in the experiences of Edwidge and
Sandra represent exceptions rather than most cases; however, this opportunity
to challenge traditional gender roles through migration and change in class status points to an important moment where gender roles become more flexible
through necessity and families have the opportunity to rethink old patterns
of gendered labor in the household. According to Nancy Foner, "Women's labor
force participation, in other words, frequently increases husbands' participation in household work and leads to changes in the balance of power in many
immigrant families."[14]

Contrary to studies that suggest that exposure to new social structures may lead to changes in household division of labor for immigrants, I argue that Haitian women act as active agents to renegotiate gender roles in the household at times out of necessity due to a profound shift in class position upon migration.[15] As Manohar explains, "In embodying strident embedded agency, Tamil women do not overthrow the heteronormative gender order—they value it even as it constrains them and marginalizes non-normative subjectivities."[16] Similarly, for Haitian women who embody strident embedded agency, it does not always manifest as a total rejection of heteronormative gender roles. Many Haitian women uphold the heteronormative gender order in the household because their strident embedded agency is based on their historically rooted gender identities that draw from their class position. However, for some women, migration offers the opportunity to assert strident embedded agency in a way that challenges traditional gender roles.

Echoing the idea that gender roles shift upon migration to synthesize gender dynamics from the country of origin and the new national context, in an analysis of Mexican women immigrants to the United States, Emilio Parrado and Chenoa Flippen state, "The reconstruction of gender relations within the family at the place of destination is a dynamic process in which some elements brought from communities of origin are discarded, others are modified, and still others are reinforced."[17] For Haitian women immigrants abroad, shifts in gender relations take place in complex and sometimes unexpected ways. Rather than a full assimilation of values and practices in their new homes, migration serves as an opportunity to renegotiate and shift gender relations to maintain connections to Haitian culture, gain a degree of integration or cultural citizenship in their new homes, and accommodate new needs surrounding paid labor and survival.

Conclusion

Part of cultural citizenship globally involves women taking on feminized work, such as caring labor both inside and outside the home. The need to take on feminized labor outside the home remains deeply classed, whereas those near the bottom of the paid labor hierarchy find themselves in situations that necessitate gendered labor outside the home as a survival mechanism. Simultaneously, affluent women are able to hire those working-class women to perform domestic and caring labor for them. In Haiti, the participants in this study were well-to-do and had nannies, cooks, and servants to clean the home; after migrating, many of them found themselves in those very positions that they previously took for granted and to which they gave little thought. Part of cultural citizenship for Black women involves being situated in a low position within the paid labor hierarchy and being forced to work both inside and outside the home to survive.

Work as Black women in the United States situated them within cultural citizenship in a subordinate position that required most women to perform paid labor outside the home and unpaid caring labor in the household. As illustrated by Sandra and by Edwidge's parents, sometimes achieving cultural citizenship through work necessitates a reorganization of traditional, by both Haitian and host country standards, gendered divisions of labor within the home.

5

Gendered Work and Work
as Independence

> I know my mother came here; she was
> working at a university, cleaning [at
> night]. And during the day she used to
> go do day work at people's houses, like
> cleaning people's houses. On weekends
> she used to be a companion [caregiver] to
> this older guy.
> —Christine, Boston

Despite the trials associated with engaging in paid labor and taking on domestic labor often for the first time, many Haitian women expressed great pride in their work. This pride in hard work aligns with the American Dream ideology centering around the myth of meritocracy, serving as a way that Haitian women become included within the dominant ethos of the United States.

Roseline expressed the complicated nature of moving from the middle and upper classes in Haiti and relying on the labor of lower-class women, to becoming the working-class woman whom others looked down on and who supplied the labor to run society. While Roseline had maids in Haiti to take care of her basic needs, upon moving to Boston she worked as an aide in a nursing home, taking care of elderly patients. Like her mother's work as a maid, Roseline's job also involved a gendered form of caring labor.

So, when I came, I went to work . . . taking care of older people. And at that time death was, "Oh!" I would say, "So-and-so is dying," and then my coworkers would say "Oh, that's okay." And I thought, "How could people be so careless with dying?" But I understand you're in a nursing home, that's what people do. So, I didn't have that perspective and I thought those were the most careless human beings I had ever met. And also the way they would wash the people. You have that little basin, and they would put some soap and wash the people and they wouldn't go and change the water. So, they would dry the people but to me the people were still soapy. You understand, because after you put soap, you have to take off the soap. So, that took longer. It would take me longer to do my patients because I did rinse them and stuff like that. So, I didn't like that.

Roseline spoke of both the class shock of performing caring labor for the first time and the culture shock of how the elderly were treated in Boston. Though as someone who grew up in the middle class in Haiti she was unfamiliar with the caring labor required of working-class women in the United States, her values as a Haitian woman meant respect for the elderly, which she applied to her job working in the nursing home. For her, that entailed respect for death and the dying, as well bathing the elderly with care rather than hastily rushing through the job.

Roseline worked for nine months before going to college. While attending college, she worked as a nurse's aide on the weekends to support herself and pay her tuition. After college and some additional training as a secretary at a Boston hospital, Roseline secured a job with an insurance company, where she excelled and easily earned promotions through the ranks. She was initially disappointed to learn that even though in the hiring process they explicitly looked for applicants with a college degree, she found that she could have done her first job with the company with only her high school math training from Haiti. While Roseline's early jobs in Boston consisted of low-status, gendered forms of caring labor, through education and her job with the insurance company, she was able to work her way back up to the middle class.

Gendered Work

Haitian men and women experience work differently upon migrating. For some Haitian women, their gender served as an asset when looking for work abroad, as many employers in the United States were seeking cheap feminine labor for housekeeping and even factory work during the first wave of migration. The ways in which certain jobs are gendered, such as how caring labor is typically considered women's work and is therefore underpaid and often relegated to women of color, shaped the access that Haitian men and women had to particular jobs.[1]

Christine illustrated the way that many Haitian women, at least initially, found themselves in gendered, low-wage labor after migrating by describing her first jobs:

> My first, first, first job ... again, it was on Saturdays. I went to serve food at a nursing home. Someone was working there ... I guess I ... a family member, or a friend of a family member that put me there and they gave me one, well, a few hours on a Saturday. So, it was through somebody. And my second job, it was like us friends after school—all of us went and we worked together.
>
> NC: What was that job?
> C: It was at the, the, the ... a factory, I guess. A wig company. We used to fix the wigs and put them in boxes. We used to wear them [laughs]. Yes, after school, and it was in South Boston, which was like doing the busing. It was ... another challenge.

Though Christine had lived in the United States for a few years before she started working in Boston, her first jobs followed the pattern consisting of low-status, racialized, and gendered labor. While working at a nursing home, she engaged in caring labor the likes of which she would not have been expected to do had she remained in Haiti. At the wig factory, Christine and her fellow young Haitian women employees worked for a white man in what was then a predominantly white, working-class neighborhood of Boston during the tense and potentially dangerous period of busing in Boston. They were most likely sought out as cheap and disposable labor because they were young Black women and immigrants.

When asked if it was easier for Haitian men or women to migrate to the United States, Christine responded,

> Ah ... I would say women ... it would be easier for women because ... women tend to, they'll try anything. I mean, like us. We'll go and do any kind of job, but men, to me, not so much. They think, especially Haitian men, you know? [laughs] So, well, I cannot say that. Some of them when they come here, they are the only person who is supporting a whole family, they'll do things too. But, to me, it's still the women will do more. And it's usually you'll see that the Haitian women are the ones that migrated first, then men, the father.
> . . .
> My father died when I was five months in my mother's belly, so my mother was always the head of the family. So, I know my mother came here; she was

working at a university, cleaning. And during the day she used to go do day work at people's houses, like cleaning people's houses. On weekends she used to be a companion [caregiver] to this older guy. So, women will do, it was easier for them to find this type of jobs, I think . . . but for women it was easier to get this kind of cleaning job. It was more available to them.

Christine remarked that at least in the context of Boston, the available jobs were gendered forms of labor such as cleaning, allowing Haitian women to find work with relative ease, although it is essential to note again the type of work Haitian women engaged in post-migration. They frequently took low-wage, low-status jobs that were typically considered to be women's work. These are jobs that they never would have taken in Haiti but that they were forced to accept in Boston because of the power differential between Haiti and the United States and because of forces of sexist racism that situated them near the bottom of the paid labor hierarchy. This power differential leads to a devaluation of Haitian credentials that migrants bring with them, and through migration they are funneled into a particular gendered labor regime. Black women in the United States have been historically relegated to devalued work, including domestic work and factory work.[2] Many Haitian women in Boston found their first jobs in these undervalued sectors where Black women in the United States have been sequestered for over a century.

Similarly, Mona described the type of jobs that Haitian men and women do upon migrating as very gendered:

Let's see. [long pause] Well, I know the job that I took when I was in high school, a lot of the guys that I knew wouldn't do it, because I know that most of the Haitian men that came here ended up driving cabs versus them going and me taking that job, not because I wanted to do it, but I figured I needed to support myself. I took the cleaning job. In a sense, based on where I come from, this is not something I would have done. But being in this country, that's what you do. I think most guys, uh, yeah, they would definitely go drive a cab versus us cleaning somebody's house or somebody's office. Yeah, I don't think a lot of them would have done it.

Mona acknowledges the shift in class position when she says, "Based on where I am from, this is not something I would have done. But being in this country, that's what you do." Many Haitian women in Boston during the first wave of migration mention taking cleaning jobs or factory work soon after migrating. According to this group of women, men were less likely to take cleaning jobs, presumably because cleaning is a gendered form of labor typically reserved for women. Cleaning jobs were available to Haitian migrants, and

Haitian women took advantage of that opportunity to provide for themselves and their families.

In addition to Haitian men and women taking different jobs than they previously may have had upon migration, scholar Mary Waters asserts that immigrants in the United States often take different types of jobs than Americans. Waters writes that immigrants accept low-wage, low-status jobs more readily than those who are native born because for immigrants their self-worth is not derived from the job in the same way. Immigrants look at jobs, including low-status jobs, in reference to the opportunities within their countries of origin.[3] While immigrants may more often accept low-wage, low-status jobs, Waters's explanation appears incomplete, as she does not address the question of why immigrants may not derive their sense of selves from their employment in the same way that natives might.

Silvia Pedraza provides an analysis of migration and employment that further complicates Waters's claims with regard to immigrants and their willingness to accept low-wage, low-status jobs. According to Pedraza, permanent immigrants work to gain social mobility by taking big risks and setting up long-term investments in family businesses.[4] In contrast to Waters, Pedraza distinguishes between temporary and permanent immigrants when examining the types of jobs immigrants may hold, implying that immigrants who view their position in a nation as temporary may attach less of a sense of self-worth to what they perceive to be a temporary, low-status job.

While temporary immigrants may not associate sense of self with employment, permanent immigrants may understand employment differently. Therefore, Haitian women intending to return to Haiti shortly may not feel the need to negotiate their identities in favor of higher-status jobs because they may primarily derive their identities in terms of their position in Haiti, rather than their position in the United States. However, Haitian women intending to stay in the United States for an extended period of time, such as the women I interviewed, may feel more invested in finding ways to mitigate the racism they experience in the United States and negotiate a higher status in American society through cultural inclusion.

Though the women in Paris did not report taking cleaning and factory jobs, some of them similarly found themselves working in low-status jobs that are often thought of as women's work. Several of the Haitian women in Paris engaged in the traditionally gendered labor of working with small children in day care centers. In Paris, Beatrice was in her early fifties, with dark skin and short, black, straightened hair that stood up in different directions. Around the roots, her hair was not straightened, and it was graying around the edges. She dressed modestly in a matching green outfit with floral print. Unlike the majority of women in this study who were from Port-au-Prince, Haiti, Beatrice was originally from Jacmel, a coastal town in the south of Haiti. She worked as a teacher there prior to migrating. Her husband moved to Paris as a political refugee under the Duvalier regime, and Beatrice soon followed with their son. Beatrice was twenty-six years old at the time. Initially, Beatrice's residence permit did not allow her to work outside the home, so she occupied herself as a stay-at-home mother for the first several years. She had another child and worked with the children at the start of the day before school and helped them with their homework in the evenings. In those early years when she could not work, she felt as though she could not do anything, and she deeply missed Haiti. She wanted to be a social worker, but her schooling in Haiti did not qualify her. She would have needed to retake exams in France comparable to what she had already passed in Haiti. It would have been very difficult, so she let go of that dream. After gaining citizenship, eventually she passed a test to be able to work at a nursery. She remarked that dealing with the adults was more challenging than dealing with the children. The nursery was understaffed, causing some friction in the workplace. Her colleagues included white French women, Algerian women, and women from southern Africa. When asked about her work at the nursery, Beatrice said, "Sometimes it's thirty or forty [children] maximum. There were six of us educators, and the nurse and the director always. There was a waiting list. The peculiar part [is that we] understand the parents. Sometimes if the parent arrives late repeatedly, the nurseries call the police. That wasn't the case with us. It's because of public transport that the mothers arrive sweating, but the director said, 'No, don't worry.' I like her, though she wasn't French but Italian, French, and German." At the nursery where Beatrice worked, she explained that employees expressed care and understanding toward the parents as well as the children by giving parents a bit of grace when they were late to pick up their children. She mentioned other nurseries calling the police in such an instance, but she was proud to report that her place of work did not resort to such tactics, adding that public transportation was typically the culprit, not the mothers who were hurrying to pick up their children.

While individual experiences illustrate the gendered nature of employment for Haitian women in diaspora, looking at the gender roles and distribution of power in Haitian-centered groups and organizations in the three field sites also sheds light on the ways in which gender roles are socially constructed and shaped by context. Asosiyasyon Fanm Ayisyen nan Boston (AFAB), a small Haitian women's organization in Boston, was unsurprisingly run by Haitian women. In Montreal, Maison d'Haïti is a large cultural center that caters to the needs of the Haitian community. Maison d'Haïti was founded by Haitian women and has a long history of strong women's leadership. In contrast, Haitian groups that I observed in Paris were largely led by Haitian men. One instance was an open house for the Haitian Catholic group, which was led by a Haitian priest. Shaped by the norms of Catholicism, the male priest sat at the front of the room with a microphone, controlling the flow of the event and using it as an opportunity to criticize the behavior of some members of the community. Many women were present at the event, quietly tending to children and distributing refreshments while the priest droned on. When the priest signaled that it was time to break for lunch, a handful of Haitian women sprang into action, taking charge in clearing the area around where they were handling the food and making up plates. Though women held some administrative roles within the organization, at this event, Haitian women were reduced to their roles as supporting members of the group, responsible for the heavily gendered tasks of caring for children and preparing food while a Haitian man sat at the helm directing and critiquing everyone else's activity. The Catholic Church as a patriarchal institution reinforces traditional gender roles that dictate that men lead, and women provide caring labor.

This gendered division of labor is perhaps expected in the Catholic organization, but the gendered dynamics between men, women, and work in the Haitian diaspora in Paris extended beyond the case of the Catholic organization. At a conference that I attended on the Haitian diaspora, the main organizers of the conference were all Haitian men. Once again, Haitian women were relegated to selling coffee and taking lunch orders.

This gendered distribution of labor in Haitian organizations in Paris speaks to gender norms in France as well as gender norms in Haiti that have, in part, been derived from the influence of French colonial rule as well as the Catholic Church. In Boston and Montreal, where there has been a greater influx of Haitian migrants, we see a disruption of traditional Western gender roles in that Haitian women take on prominent roles in cultural organizations rather than relying on patriarchal structures as we see in the case of the Catholic Haitian association in Paris. While Haitian women still take on gendered work in the household and in typically female occupations such as cleaning and nursing, in Boston and Montreal, Haitian women also come together as community leaders.

Perhaps the leadership of Haitian women in cultural organizations in Boston and Montreal harkens back to the role of Haitian women in Vodou. Unlike in the Catholic Church, both men and women serve as priests in the Vodou religion. In Haiti there is a saying, "Fanm se poto mitan," meaning that women are the pillars of society. "Poto mitan" literally references the pillar in the center of a Vodou temple, which signifies connecting the earthly world to the spiritual realm. In the case of Haitian organizations in Boston and Montreal, we see Haitian women living up to the adage that Haitian women are the pillars of society. In secular Haitian community organizations in Boston and Montreal, Haitian women serve as the "poto mitan" for the community, providing resources and social support for others while also carrying on Haitian culture to the next generations. It is common for nations even outside of the Haitian context to view women as the keepers of culture and tradition. However, Haitian women in organizations in Boston and Montreal have taken that charge and mobilized as community leaders rather than doing the work of cultural reproduction solely in the private sphere of the home.

Haitian women are constrained by social forces around them but are by no means powerless actors. As Mary Beth Mills writes about young Thai women undergoing rural-urban migration to engage in factory labor, "They are neither victims pure and simple nor free and unfettered actors. Rather, they must be understood as conscious agents, making decisions and pursuing goals within—and, at times, despite—their often difficult circumstances."[5] This quote from Mills resonates with Aihwa Ong's description of people in diaspora as "active manipulators of cultural symbols."[6] Haitian women face the entwined forces of sexism and racism in Haitian society and in their host societies. As Haitians, they are also situated particularly within the global political economy as workers from a nation-state that has historically undergone serious exploitation and has been rendered economically weak and vulnerable on the global stage. Though forced to contend with racism and sexism in the workplace as they are frequently directed into gendered forms of paid labor, Haitian women maintain agency as they navigate these challenges. One way that Haitian women exercise agency in the Boston context is by aligning themselves with normative American ideology surrounding work to ease their cultural integration into U.S. society.

Work as Independence

As discussed in chapter 4, Haitian women in Boston reference both sides of the debate of whether work is empowering or oppressive for women, and for Black women in particular. Since these women recognize the burdens of engaging in paid labor while shouldering other responsibilities and the financial autonomy they derive from paid labor, their narratives support both sides of the debate. However, their experiences do more than simply support existing dialogue about whether paid labor is oppressive or empowering for women. By highlighting the importance of work in their experiences, regardless of its emancipatory nature, Marie, Judeline, Bernadette, and Esther in particular draw attention to the centrality of work in terms of belonging and identity formation. Work gave these women a sense of independence from their parents and husbands, allowed them to participate directly in the national economies of their host country and Haiti, and provided them with social connections in their new national context.

By working outside the home, Haitian women migrants, especially the older generation who migrated in the 1960s and 1970s, gained a degree of economic independence not previously enjoyed in Haiti, allowing them to participate directly in national economies rather than relying on the incomes of their parents or husbands. They participated in the nation in different ways than they previously had as their gendered and classed positions in society shifted.

Paid labor as a source of independence and pride emerged as a recurring theme among participants, particularly for women in the first wave of migration to Boston. Despite the difficult and low-wage labor they found themselves performing, they valued both their work, and the new degree of autonomy from their parents or partners that it afforded them. This excitement over the opportunity to work as a way to gain autonomy from parents and husbands is a uniquely gendered phenomenon in that Haitian men were typically expected to work prior to migration, whereas middle- and upper-class Haitian women in the 1960s and 1970s often felt that migration presented them with the opportunity, albeit also the necessity, to work outside the home for the first time.

Now a middle-aged woman with light-brown skin and straightened hair, Marie recounted her experience of immigrating to Boston from Haiti in 1970 at the age of fifteen. Marie moved to Boston with her siblings to be reunited with their mother, who had been living and working in the United States for a couple of years at that point. Though Marie's family lived a comfortable middle-class lifestyle in Haiti with domestic laborers to help with the cooking and cleaning, after migrating to the United States, her mother struggled to provide for all of her children. Marie decided to get a job to alleviate some of the economic pressure on her family but also to gain some amount of financial independence. She said, "I got a job when I was sixteen, cleaning offices in Boston. I said, 'One day I will have an office and someone else will clean my office.'" Though Marie accepted a gendered and low-status job, she aspired to one day reclaim the status that she had left in Haiti by once again hiring someone else to clean for her.

Marie explained that juggling schoolwork and a job was no easy feat: "Trying to work so I had money and trying to stay awake. I took [caffeine pills,] but I slept right through it. It was a quick growing up. We had lots of homework in Haiti, but this time I'm trying to work and go to school at the same time and my family wasn't quite the way it used to be."

Despite the hardships, Marie eagerly discussed the benefits of moving to the United States. When asked what the best part of moving to the United States was for her, Marie enthusiastically replied, "Opportunities! I kept thinking, 'I'm going to go to college!' That was great. I was able to work and get money in my pockets. In Haiti, there were no jobs." Though Marie did not work while attending school in Port-au-Prince, Haiti, she envisioned that working in Boston would provide her with the educational and career opportunities that were previously inaccessible to her. For Marie, paid labor, despite hardships and low status, offered her as a young woman a new level of independence and a steppingstone to a future where she would achieve higher class status and once again rely on the paid labor of lower-class women.

Judeline was forty years old when I interviewed her in 2011 and had migrated to Boston from Haiti with her sister when she was twenty-nine. I spent time with her in her modest two-story home in a middle-class suburb of Boston. She was running about an hour late to meet me, leaving me plenty of time to observe her quiet, residential, tree-lined street. Judeline arrived home that evening flustered, with her five-year-old son in tow. She hurriedly set her son up with dinner in front of the television before joining me in the dining room to talk. She had a pile of textbooks next to her at the dining room table, and later told me that in addition to working full-time as a certified nursing assistant and raising her son, she was studying sociology at a local college. Though she is younger than the women of the first wave of migration in this study, Judeline expressed similar feelings regarding work as a source of autonomy that she had not experienced in Haiti: "It was like, a great experience. I mean by great, like okay, back home, you know, you live with your parents. It's like they have control over you, but I came here; it's like I was by myself, you know? So . . . that's why I said it was a great experience, you know?"

Judeline described working post-migration as key to freedom from her parents' control. In some ways work and migration translate into less gendered surveillance in the family. As a young woman in Haiti, she felt beholden to her parents due to societal expectations based on her gender and class. Upon moving to Boston, she was forced to work to support herself. Though it was difficult to find a job at first because of her limited English language skills, her niece, who had lived in Boston for five years already at that point, helped her go to various locations to fill out applications. Eventually, she landed her first job cleaning at the conference center of a small college in the Boston area. In the interview, she said yes to everything her future employer said to her, trying to make herself an attractive candidate by portraying a positive, if subservient, attitude. When asked what the best part about migrating was, Judeline replied, "To be free! [laughter] That was the only best part."

For Judeline, working as a Black woman in the United States signified freedom from prior societal constraints she experienced when living in Haiti with her family. By making herself amenable to any tasks or requests her future employer may have had, she accepted her placement near the bottom of the paid labor hierarchy. Though deeply problematic that as a Black woman she needed to accept any and all working conditions no matter how poor, her acceptance of her place in the paid labor hierarchy enabled her to pay for her own housing and expenses, a level of independence previously unknown to her as a middle-class woman in Haiti. A middle-class lifestyle meant a degree of luxury but also dependence on others. Being able to provide for herself meant self-efficacy and independence.

Bernadette, who was introduced in chapter 2, was young and lacked any prior work experience when she arrived in the United States. Bernadette's work in those early years consisted of low-wage, "unskilled" positions. Despite the low status of her jobs, Bernadette felt passionately about working and gaining the ability to send money to her family in Haiti:

> My first job, it was a factory. They were making makeup. So, I was in the line, assembly. I didn't have anything, nothing, no training or anything. So, I went there. I did that and they were paying forty dollars a week. And at the time, forty dollars was a lot of money, because we could go to shopping with fifteen dollars and you buy everything with fifteen dollars. . . . I could have some money to send to my family, too, I could send a little money. There, [my husband's] not going to give me money to send to them. Because he doesn't want the money to go there to them so they can come. He didn't want nobody to come around me. I was always forceful with myself. I always wanted to go to work. I went and worked there a few months. And I was taking care of my kids . . . but I had a good time going to work. Because there are people, friends.

She later moved to Boston, where she lived, worked, and continued to raise a family. When asked what she considered to be the easiest or best part of moving to the United States, Bernadette replied, "The easiest part about moving here? I never thought of it. You can do whatever you want. You can do whatever you like. That's the thing. If I say I want to do this, I just go and do it. If I say I want to go and work there, and I go there and work. And I worked someplace, and I was the boss. I looked for people to work for me, to come and work. I like it. You can do what you want to."

When asked how her life has changed since moving to the United States, Christine, who previously shared about her early work experiences in a nursing home and in a wig factory, paused for a long time before replying:

> [long pause] Well, now I went to school, I got better jobs, you know. And I have a better husband, so my life is much better now since I can express myself. You know? And, actually my job they really think a lot of me. Because I always tell them, "Yeah, yeah. But the way I deal with people, it's because of my background. You respect people and things like that." So, from when I just got here to now, my life has improved socially, financially. Everything is better now, but I still wish I could be home. [laughs]

> NC: When you say that you can express yourself now, is that just language, or do you feel a difference in terms of like empowerment?

C: Empowerment, no, it's not just the language barrier. But, you know, I can stand up and to any Haitian I can say, "No, we can do this, we can do that." Just because sometimes they say, "Oh yeah, okay." No.

NC: What do you think has enabled you to do that? What has changed?

C: Well, now, because of all the women . . . women . . . women have always had and now can express themselves and by going to social women's things you listen and then you see, you know, I get empowered. I say, "Now I can stand up and do this. I don't have to be, you know, the submissive person anymore." Yeah, you know?

Christine identified her professional advancements as key factors contributing to feeling able to express herself as a woman. She emphasized that they think very highly of her at work, contrasting her current position as a manager for a technology company with the low-status labor that so many Haitian women in the Boston area performed initially after migrating. The fact that she was respected and well-regarded at work helped Christine to navigate her cultural citizenship and led to an increased sense of belonging in the nation.

Esther, a warm, talkative, and deeply religious woman in her early sixties with medium-light skin and natural hair pulled back in a tight low bun, grew up in Haiti helping take care of the household even though her family had maids; she also pursued a career in Haiti with UNESCO as a young woman. When I first met her, she greeted me with a big hug before any introductions. She was unemployed and volunteering part-time for a nonprofit in Boston when I met her, having been laid off from her job the previous year. Esther's mother felt strongly that her daughters should know how to sew, cook, and clean, while Esther's brothers were not required to partake in any of these household tasks. Esther explained that though she grew up learning how to take care of the household, she was not prepared to be confined to the house once she married in Haiti at the age of twenty-one:

Because of my husband, my life had been hell. I wasn't prepared for that. I was prepared by my parents to be a romantic woman. That's why I know how to cook, clean, sew. And how to be a good mother and good wife, but that doesn't mean slavery! That doesn't mean housewife. I'm a professional. I can go out and share my money and wealth with my husband and kids. That was my dream. But that guy turned my dream away from me. I said to myself, maybe it was a dream. Maybe he was only a dream and never been reality.

He made me stop working as a matter of fact. When he came to me, he was an angel. Once we got married and I moved out and didn't live with my mom anymore, I remember that after one month, because I took one month leave of absence [from work] thinking that would be okay. When I was ready to go back to work he said, "No, not my wife. I've got a job. You've got to stay home. Take care of me." I said, "Excuse me?" This was the first impression I had of that guy. He was a tall guy. In front of him I was just little. Tall and handsome guy. Very light skin and nice hair. Pretty and very educated. But he was a monster.

Eventually with the help of her brother who lived in the United States, Esther was able to escape her abusive marriage and move to the United States, where she regained a sense of independence and returned to working outside the home again. Esther moved around the United States and worked for various companies before settling at a mutual fund in Boston:

It was the first mutual fund in Massachusetts. They train you in mutual fund accounting. Numbers, money, big money. I mostly did office jobs, you know. I said, "Mom, I'm going to be permanent on May 18." Let's say he called me, today is Monday, it was the next Monday. [My new boss] had already set up everything to pay the temp agency. I spent thirteen years there. They paid for school for me. That's why I have a degree in finance and engineering. In Haiti there is a private engineering program that my parents can't afford and you couldn't go to the state one because it was political under Duvalier. Engineering is in my blood and accounting is because I couldn't afford it. I couldn't be what I really wanted to be since in Haiti, so I worked for UNESCO. I did filing [in the United States]. I still wasn't an engineer. They sent me to school; I graduated; I was so happy. Free.

Esther's job with the mutual fund allowed her to pursue her education and earn a degree in engineering, a longtime dream of hers, for free. Though Esther prided herself on her identity as a working professional, work has not always been easy for her. She has struggled as a substitute teacher in Boston public schools and she expressed how difficult it was as an older Black woman in Boston to find a job that suited her skills after being laid off, leading to an extended period of unemployment. Esther experienced racism and sexism in hiring as they intersected with the force of ageism as well.

When discussing the challenges of racism and sexism while working in Boston, one woman made passing reference to being subjected to serious sexual harassment in the workplace. Fabienne was in her fifties but looked much younger. With medium-dark skin and straightened shoulder-length hair, she was always sharply dressed. Fabienne initially moved to Montreal at age thirteen and to Boston at age seventeen. When asked about her first jobs in Boston, she replied,

Where did I work . . . I don't even remember . . . maybe a bridal shop, I think? No, it was like a house of couture. My uncle was working there as a tailor or something like that and got me a job in a department where they handle all the different patterns. I was there for about eight months and then I encountered some major sexual harassment from an older Italian man who was very, very fresh and inappropriate. I was twenty-one at the time. That's another long story. So I left. Then I started to . . . I ended up doing some office work here and there, maybe as a secretary and started to go to school part time. I ended up renting my own little apartment right next door to my family because I needed the help and support with my daughter. I started to go to school part time and to work in different offices with different jobs.

After taking various jobs to make ends meet, Fabienne eventually earned her bachelor's degree from a prestigious college in the Boston area and became the founder and director of her own nonprofit. For Fabienne, work was a means to an end at first, providing her with the money necessary to take care of her young daughter after leaving her first husband and exposing her to sexual harassment. Over time and with increased experience and education, work became a major part of her identity.

Marie, Judeline, Bernadette, Christine, and Esther each offered narratives that emphasize the potentially emancipatory aspect of paid labor. However, despite their pride in work and economic independence, Marie and Bernadette highlight the ways in which work served as a burden as well. Marie needed to take caffeine pills in an attempt to tackle schoolwork and working long hours. Judeline was visibly frazzled and tired from working full-time while raising her young son and trying to pursue her studies. For Bernadette, work put a strain on her already abusive marriage, but she wanted to work in order to provide for her family in Haiti while taking care of her children in the United States.

For these Haitian women, work played a complicated role in their lives, subjecting them to forces of racism and sexism while simultaneously providing them with a source of economic independence and even a sense of identity in some cases. By adopting, at least in part, the American Dream ideology, many Boston-based Haitian women in this study expressed great pride in their work, situating themselves as cultural citizens of the United States.

Conclusion

Though frequently tracked into gendered forms of labor, many women in this study cited work as a key to independence and a source of pride, particularly in the Boston context. Gendered labor set Haitian women within the social and economic hierarchies of the nation as their participation in these forms of labor illustrate how dominant norms surrounding race and gender play out in the workplace through the types of work available to Haitian women. In the

Boston context, the pride Haitian women expressed in work resonates with the American Dream ideology. This alignment with dominant U.S. ideology, whether consciously or subconsciously, marks these women as cultural citizens of the United States in a meaningful way, though that inclusion in the nation and in the workforces continues to be shaped by forces of racism and sexism. In this way, belief in the American Dream as it relates to hard work inevitably reaping rewards becomes a clear point of national inclusion for immigrants in the United States despite the fact that Haitian women are forced into labor hierarchies that are frequently oppressive toward women, particularly women of color.

6

All Work Is Cultural Work

Karine, a thin and fit Haitian woman in her mid-thirties with curly natural hair, teaches dance in Montreal to both Canadian and Haitian students. She moved to Montreal as a young adult after her mother was held at gunpoint outside of Karine's dance school in Haiti. At the time of the interview, Karine lived with her mother in a modest home in Montreal, and her mother helped out with Karine's fitness center and dance studio. The dance course Karine teaches is advertised as Haitian folkloric dance, though the choreography is clearly infused with aspects of contemporary dance. In teaching Haitian dance in Montreal, Karine is doing important cultural work in re-creating Haiti in diaspora. As such, part of the national culture is made outside the nation-state. The class serves as a meeting place for Haitians to celebrate their culture and is open to people of all nationalities who would like to study Haitian dance formally as an art form. Karine also organizes dance performances on occasion to share the art form with the larger Montreal community, thereby making Haitian culture a visible and celebrated part of Quebec. In this way, the dance teacher is a cultural worker doubly over.

In this chapter I examine how Haitian women in diaspora create and re-create multiple national contexts in the course of their paid labor. This analysis sheds light on the experiences of individual women that point to broader local, national, and transnational sociological processes. This culminating chapter examines national belonging as a form of cultural citizenship, using the concept of cultural work to highlight the complex relationship between labor and belonging in the nation. Cultural work relates to citizenship in that it provides the labor that creates and maintains the nation; cultural work is an act of cultural citizenship in that it illustrates one's place within the national context. Using cultural work as a lens of analysis, I assert that workplace interactions shape national identity in the daily negotiation of cultural values, norms, and behaviors that indicate who belongs within various national contexts.

Cultural Workers

Through my ethnographic fieldwork in the metropolitan areas of Boston, Montreal, and Paris, I gained insights into the experiences of individual women that point to local, national, and transnational sociological processes. The women with whom I interacted for this study occupied a wide range of professions: novelists, community organizers, dance teachers, social workers, fitness coaches, and nursery school educators, among others. For some of these professions, such as those in creative fields, the link between paid labor and cultural work seems apparent in that they produce widely recognizable cultural products. From a Marxist perspective, work necessarily involves alienation, or the process by which the laborer puts part of themselves into the products they produce. When Haitian women abroad create art, those cultural products are imbued with the creator's multi- and transnational identities and experiences. Those cultural products may be consumed by Haitians and non-Haitians, and in the creation of those products, the artists contribute to the making of Haitian national identity as well as enriching the culture of their adoptive nations.

Scholars of gender and nation have documented the ways in which women are frequently expected to act as symbols of national identity, being both the holders of tradition and those responsible for passing on culture to the next generation.[1] In Haiti, high value is placed on mulatto women in the upper classes as symbolic carriers of European-descendent culture, while women in the working class make up almost half of the workforce.[2] In fact, some scholars have argued that because of women's prominent role as respected leaders in Vodou and the strong female literary tradition in Haiti, women play a more prominent role in Haitian national culture than women in other nations.[3] Haitian women abroad do that cultural work of creating and maintaining the nation for Haiti as well as for their adoptive nations. For instance, Karine, by engaging in cultural work as a form of paid labor, integrates herself into Quebec's economy and earns enough money to send remittances to her family members who remain in Haiti. She develops a social network in Quebec through the people with whom she comes into contact while teaching dance. She also maintains close relationships with her family and friends in Haiti through frequent digital communication and yearly visits. Clearly, Karine's work therefore ties her culturally and economically to two national contexts.

Canada's multicultural approach to integrating immigrants eases Karine's cultural integration through her work as a dancer by celebrating cultural difference and inviting cultural minorities to share their cultures as part of the multicultural fabric of the nation. The presence of Maison d'Haïti supports the visibility of the Haitian community in Montreal and provides an opportunity for Haitian professionals such as Karine to network and collaborate. Additionally, Quebec's complicated relationship with its French-Canadian heritage makes francophone immigrants like Karine more attractive than anglophone immigrants who might threaten Quebec's linguistic identity. Though Karine's Blackness differentiates her from the dominant French-Canadian population in Quebec, the backdrop of Canada's multicultural approach to integration allows space for Karine to practice and share her Haitian culture; however, deep-seated beliefs about who truly belongs in the nation (i.e., white French Canadians) at times seeps through in Quebec's nationalist discourse. While her identity as a Black migrant worker still positions her in particular ways within the nation, Karine gains a degree of cultural inclusion through her paid labor. Through her paid labor she is able to negotiate a place for herself within the nation as a Black foreign woman.

I use this example of a dance teacher to illustrate the ways in which paid labor serves as an important point at which Haitian women forge cultural and economic ties to the nation; however, I assert that all paid work is cultural work. A social worker and a teacher of English as a second language similarly serve as cultural workers through their daily interactions with a range of people from numerous nationalities.

Bernice Johnson Reagon, civil rights activist and self-proclaimed cultural worker, proposes that culture is more than a product to be consumed and analyzed; Reagon understands culture as a methodology and as "an analysis of the conditions of Black people in the larger world."[4] In this chapter, I use specific examples from my fieldwork with Haitian women across national contexts to illustrate how their paid labor shapes, in small but meaningful ways, the nations around them.

To illustrate how we can use the lens of cultural work to understand all paid labor, I present two additional examples from my fieldwork. First, in Boston, a Haitian woman named Edwidge works as an administrative assistant in a large hospital. Edwidge is a sharp, impeccably dressed woman in her mid-fifties who gives off a professional air. She moved to Boston when she was sixteen years old, following her parents who migrated for economic reasons four years prior, her mother taking up employment as a nanny and her father as a welder. At work, Edwidge is in charge of scheduling patients for surgeries and consultations and interacts with dozens of people from all walks of life in the office each day. In her countless phone calls and meetings with patients, she proudly displays respect and professionalism, traits that she attributes to her Haitian upbringing.

In the hospital, she is frequently called upon to serve as a volunteer translator for Haitian patients, even for patients outside of her department. People know that she is Haitian, and when they find themselves in a situation where they have a Haitian patient and no family member present to translate, they call on her to step in. She likes to help other Haitians when she can because she feels empathy for their struggles, but she tells me with frustration in her voice that though hospitals are required to provide translators, too often, patients do not know they are able to request translation services. Her demeanor as she tells me about the difficulties Haitian patients face indicates that she feels protective of her fellow Haitians and is displeased with the dominant culture in Boston hospitals, which treats Haitians as less deserving of quality care. As a well-respected member of the hospital staff, she uses her Haitian identity and language skills to do unpaid translation services to benefit both the hospital and Haitian patients.

While the type of work she performs differs from Karine's work as a dance teacher, paid labor similarly ties Edwidge to multiple national contexts affectively and economically. Edwidge is able to send remittances and visit family and friends in Haiti every few years. Though Edwidge does not visit Haiti very often, her elderly parents live in Haiti and visit Boston yearly for routine medical care. Edwidge's salary enables her to help her parents pay for these trips and sometimes for costly medical care. Additionally, her connections within the hospital expose her to information about how and where to get the best health care for her aging parents within the city's many hospitals.

Outside of work, Edwidge primarily socializes with other Haitians in the Boston area, many of whom she has known for decades. She is not involved with any official Haitian organizations but informally hosts a small group of Haitians (primarily Haitian women) at her home every Friday evening where they eat Haitian food, speak Haitian Kreyòl, and laugh into the night. The group members keep each other up to date on everything from the latest gossip among their mutual acquaintances to the current political situation in Haiti. Edwidge's work during the day at the hospital puts her into daily contact with non-Haitians, making her into the fabric of the hospital's cultural landscape. When she is outside of work, her income allows her the leisure time to socialize with her Haitian friends. This leisure time on Friday nights is a microsite at which the Haitian national identity is re-created and maintained in Boston.

Like Montreal, Boston exists within a nation with a multicultural approach to integration, allowing for Edwidge to identify as a Haitian woman within the American context while still making a place for herself within the nation. Like Karine, her identity as a Black woman situates her within the nation in particular ways, at times limiting her degree of inclusion within the nation.

As a Black woman in the 1970s in Boston, Edwidge got her first job when she was in high school, in a factory working with other young Haitian women, one of the only jobs available to her as a young Black woman at that time. She found the position through her informal Haitian diasporic social networks, the same networks that supported her as she pursued higher education and moved into middle-class work. Edwidge has actively participated in these informal networks, an important piece of Boston's sociopolitical landscape, from the time she first arrived in Boston and worked in lower-class jobs to the present moment when she now plays a central role in maintaining those networks in her leisure time. As a Black woman, Edwidge at times experiences marginalization within the nation in terms of residential segregation and her situation within labor hierarchies; however, her paid labor supports her financially, puts her in daily contact with others in the nation, and allows her to use aspects of her identity as a Haitian woman to succeed professionally. Her identity and linguistic skills as a Haitian woman prove to be an asset in the workplace. Also, her strong work ethic, a highly touted Haitian trait, makes her an invaluable member of her team at work.

Lastly, Wideline worked as a nursery school teacher in a suburb of Paris for many years until she had to stop due to an injury. Wideline is a tall and strong woman with medium-brown skin who always speaks slowly using excessively formal and flowery language. As a state-employed teacher, she worked with small children, often spending more waking hours with them than their own parents did. Through her caring labor, she taught toddlers how to interact socially and what behavior was expected of them. In short, she taught them how to be "good" citizens who could thrive in French society because of their cultural knowledge. Though most of the children were French-born, some of their parents were immigrants. As an employee of a state-run nursery, Wideline was responsible for transmitting French national culture to the children; though by nature of her upbringing, Wideline invariably also passed along Haitian cultural values of respect and acceptable behavior as well.

Now Wideline works as an administrator in a government office in the suburb outside Paris where she resides. She is the only Haitian employee in her office. She uses the same cultural values of respect that she previously taught to French children in her interactions with coworkers in her office job. Still working as an employee of the government, she represents the French nation in her interactions with those who encounter her at work.

Outside of work, Wideline is very involved with her Haitian church group, serving on its board and organizing church gatherings. The church group is a Haitian-only space where all proceedings take place in Haitian Kreyòl. In addition to religious worship, the group organizes to send relief aid to Haiti following natural disasters.

Given France's assimilationist approach to immigrant integration and the much smaller number of Haitian immigrants in Paris, Wideline does not interact with other Haitians in the workplace on a regular basis. She is seen as French before all else and becomes an ambassador for French culture as though it is possible to erase her identity as a Haitian woman while at work. As a result, the cultural inclusion that Wideline achieves through work is that of a French citizen who is stripped of any other cultural identity, though in reality, her upbringing in Haiti and Haitian cultural values surrounding respect and proper comportment color all her workplace interactions. In this way, Wideline shapes and redefines French culture through her daily workplace interactions, though that work remains largely invisible in the context of assimilationist politics. Though France as a nation does not support the maintenance of prior national identities, Wideline has found fellowship with other Haitians through her religious community, where they maintain Haitian culture through language, social activities, and cuisine.

France espouses a color-blind ideology in which race is not explicitly acknowledged, but the ideal French citizen remains white in the national imagination. Wideline is able to mediate the exclusion from Frenchness that she faces as a Black woman by serving as a cultural ambassador for France in her micro, daily, workplace interactions. While her race and nation of origin may place her outside of French national inclusion despite France's allegedly color-blind approach to integration, her role as a paid laborer for the state interpellates her as a citizen who has a place within the nation.

Inspired by Reagon's conception of cultural work as transformative, I call on this as a framework for understanding the powerfully generative aspect of the daily work of Haitian women. Rather than merely completing assigned tasks, I assert that Haitian women leave their mark on coworkers, clients, institutions, and communities, thereby shaping the national contexts in which they are embedded. Reagon's understanding of cultural work, coupled with Nina Glick Schiller and Georges E. Fouron's concept of "transnationalism from below," offers the theoretical framing necessary to augment dominant conceptions of citizenship with an analysis of how presumably marginal individuals (Black, immigrant, women) actively shape the bounds of nations.[5] According to Fouron and Schiller, individuals create and sustain transnational networks on the ground. Reagon's definitions of cultural work can thus explain *how* individuals then shape transnational processes, elucidating an oft-overlooked piece of how citizens and nations are produced.

Though most of the women with whom I spoke consider themselves fully integrated into their host societies, and in most cases are naturalized citizens of those nations, every Haitian woman I spoke to across those field sites remains affectively tied to Haiti. Following Schiller and others, I suggest that these women's experiences support a "both/and" rather than an "either/or" notion of citizenship; for these women, belonging in one national context does not exclude belonging in multiple nations. For them, Haiti is always "home," even if they emigrated decades ago and had no plans to return. Haitian women remain connected to Haiti through cultural organizations, charities, music, language, remittances, political discussions, and transnational family networks.

Some women return to Haiti to visit friends and family yearly or every few years; others have not returned since emigrating, often because they left under difficult circumstances with threats to their personal safety. Regardless of the individual relationships to current-day Haiti geographically, almost all remain connected through diasporic networks of family and friends that are dispersed across the globe but largely concentrated in New York and Florida.

These workplace interactions can be understood through the lens of cultural work that reproduces customs, traditions, and values that shape national identity. On another level, paid labor enables economic participation in multiple national contexts by providing the economic capital to send remittances to family in Haiti, make charitable donations to Haitian organizations, and engage in volunteer work to support Haitian communities abroad.

In addition to cultural work at the individual level through employment, many Haitian women in diaspora engage with organizations that perform cultural work for the Haitian community and for their host nations. The political climate of the host nation, particularly with regard to racial and ethnic diversity, influences the ways in which Haitian women create and re-create Haitian national identity abroad. Various nations conditionally accept Haitian women so long as their labor is deemed valuable. Perhaps particularly in capitalist nations, paid labor and the economy play a crucial role in determining terms of inclusion for immigrants. The need for immigrant labor shapes the conditional inclusion of certain migrants at certain points in time.[6] This conditional inclusion is frequently fraught with racism and the exploitation of migrant labor. It is also a subordinate inclusion that maintains the power of elites to determine the time, pace, and nature of inclusion.[7]

Conclusion

Haitian women in diaspora perform cultural work through their paid labor that reproduces, creates, and sustains Haitian and other national cultures and identities. A close examination of the daily experiences of Haitian women in Boston, Montreal, and Paris demonstrates the ways that paid labor serves as a site of cultural work in nation-building, focusing on processes of "transnationalism from below."[8] This bottom-up approach to examining national identity emphasizes the agency Haitian women exercise as individuals and as a collective, and reveals how the workplace serves as a micro-site where Haitian women negotiate power relations and the bounds of nation.

I assert that national belonging is created and re-created in daily interactions. Haitian women perform cultural work that is frequently undervalued and taken for granted. This study specifically examines paid labor outside the home, as the workplace serves as an important site where Haitian women come into contact with others, and fosters the environments in which culture is reproduced and transmitted through subtle daily interactions. Haitian women in diaspora are uniquely situated to illuminate the multiple processes at play in determining the boundaries of nation and the terms of inclusion, as their experiences defy classical definitions that depict nations as necessarily mutually exclusive.

The political climate, influenced by processes of the global political economy and the specificities of each national context, affects the resources available and stands as an obstacle to inclusion that Haitian women face as they negotiate national belonging. This chapter includes an overview of the meso- and macro-level forces at play to contextualize and give additional depth to the individual experiences of Haitian women; this review of those processes is meant to complement, not to overshadow or minimize, the micro-level interactions through which Haitian women creatively negotiate national belonging and thrive across the world.

The experiences of Haitian women abroad illustrate how "nation" as a category of analysis is necessary and yet inadequate. This study demonstrates how Haitian women in diaspora negotiate belonging in multiple national contexts simultaneously, complicating classical conceptions of nation-states as mutually exclusive entities. Haitian women in each of these sites are instrumental in carrying out cultural work at an organizational level; at the same time, the data show that historical context and national policies regarding racial inclusion clearly influence the ways in which Haitian communities form and organize.

Conclusion

The findings of this study are based on interviews and participant observation with Haitian women of a certain class who worked outside the home, and future studies could expand upon this research by investigating the relationships between paid labor and national belonging for working-class Haitian women and Haitian women who only work in the domestic sphere as well. Drawing from the experiences of the women in this study, I suspect that work continues to situate working-class women within the nation in particular ways but that they may feel that low-wage and low-status paid labor outside the home includes them in the nation in oppressive and contradictory ways. This was the case for some of the Haitian women who experienced a downward shift in class status initially upon migration, which necessitated they take on work as cleaning women, nannies, or factory workers. However, even those low-status jobs granted them a level of economic freedom from their parents and husbands that they did not necessarily experience in Haiti, especially for women who migrated in the 1960s and 1970s as part of the first wave of migration. Working-class women also found that work outside the home granted them important opportunities to make connections with others in the nation outside of their familial networks, situating them within the nation through those daily workplace interactions.

This study did not engage with women who exclusively perform domestic labor in their own homes or in the homes of other Haitians in diaspora. From my observations in the field, I suspect that this form of labor functions very differently when it comes to negotiating national inclusion, as it creates an insular world in the home where Haitian women are not necessarily coming into regular contact with others in the nation and therefore not doing the daily cultural work of building the nation in a direct manner. However, by raising children who do actively engage in the nation through school and eventually paid labor, Haitian women who only work within the home may still have a hand in shaping the national culture of their new homes in an indirect manner.

This project studies the relationship between paid labor and national belonging, focusing on the lived experiences of Haitian women in diaspora as a point of entry. As with the example of Karine, the Haitian dance teacher in Montreal discussed in chapter 6, the experiences of Haitian women in Boston, Montreal, and Paris enable us to look at the intersectional processes at play in terms of race, gender, and nation of origin when examining the issue of national belonging. This study in no way attempts to present the experiences of Haitian women as uniform or homogenous; rather, the diversity of Haitian women's experiences points to different aspects of the relationships between paid labor and national belonging. The varied experiences of Haitian artists, government employees, and hospital workers shed light on the ways in which national belonging operates through paid labor.

In addition to contributing to literatures on gender and migration, race, and transnationalism, this study contributes to the theorization of cultural citizenship through an analysis of paid labor and national belonging. I began this project through the process of inductive reasoning, collecting data, and allowing those data to point to patterns and build theory. Though I did not start with the concept of cultural citizenship, my data urged me to look at theories of citizenship and national belonging. Through an iterative process of data collection and analysis, I came to engage my research with theories of cultural citizenship. I ultimately found that the experiences of Haitian women could augment existing theories of cultural citizenship, reinvigorating the term and allowing for scholars to engage with it anew.

Paid labor plays a central role in negotiating cultural citizenship for Haitian women in that it situates them within the nation of arrival through their daily workplace interactions. By coming into contact with other members of the nation, Haitian women shape both the nation and their relationship to it. For instance, Wideline, the government employee in Paris discussed in chapter 6, represents the French nation while performing her job, but her performance in the workplace is always informed by her Haitian upbringing. In this way, Wideline infuses Haitian cultural values into the French nation through her workplace interactions while the workplace rules, regulations, and customs create a framework within which Wideline exerts agency. Wideline's experiences illustrate how cultural citizenship is a process of self-making and being made, a process that takes place in large part through paid labor outside the home.[1]

This study ties the micro-level daily experiences of Haitian women to macro-level processes of race, labor, and national belonging. This research highlights the back-and-forth interplay between the micro and macro levels of experience. The daily lives of Haitian women shape the macro forces of race and paid labor, while those forces create the conditions within which Haitian women exercise agency in their daily lives. Rather than pointing to a unidirectional causal relationship, this research sheds light on the cyclical relationship between micro- and macro-level processes.

The multisited focus of this study enables an analysis that addresses yet transcends the specificities of single nations, illustrating that macro-level processes exist and function transnationally. Race and ethnicity exist in each of the three field sites, though the local context inflects the manifestation of race and ethnicity in each instance. Race transcends national borders partly because of the ways in which it is tied to the dynamics of global capital. Haitians come from a country with a long history of economic exploitation that has taken place alongside the racialization of Haitians as inferior on the global stage.

The particular case of Haitian women in diaspora connects back to broader implications for understandings of race, gender, paid labor, and national belonging. The processes uncovered in this research have relevance for many members of Western, predominantly white, capitalist nations, not just migrants. The implications for other migrants of color are perhaps easiest to see; I suggest that the processes of cultural citizenship uncovered through the paid labor of migrant Haitian women play out similarly for other migrant groups in Western nations as well. I also suggest that there are implications for native-born citizens. Paid labor and cultural citizenship do not exclusively apply to migrants, since native-born members of the population are differentially situated within the nation through their paid labor as well. Just like for Haitian women, native-born citizens come into contact with certain people through their paid labor, creating opportunities to reinforce racial and ethnic boundaries within the nation. Native-born citizens also shape the nation through their daily workplace interactions, similar to the examples of the ways in which Haitian women shape the nation in this study. The case of Haitian women throws into relief some of the aspects of how people shape the nation through their paid labor because Haitian women are marginalized in terms of race, gender, and nation of origin, yet they are never completely powerless in shaping the world in which they live.

This study gives voice to a segment of the population that is often overlooked or portrayed only as deserving to be pitied to show that scholars have much to learn from Haitian women, their labor, and their resilience. Haitian women find ways not only to survive but to thrive in their new homes. Their relationships to the paid workforce are crucial to their ability to do both, since paid labor situates them within the context of the nation.

This study complements the work of scholars who focus on the role of paid labor in purely economic terms by emphasizing the fact that the cultural work of building the nation takes place in a context shaped by paid labor. As such, understandings of race and ethnicity that are forged in the workplace play an important role in shaping race and ethnicity within the nation and transnationally.

In the introduction, I laid out the reasoning as to why multisited ethnography as a method allows for the examination of cross-sections of processes that might otherwise remain difficult to see, focusing on how multisited ethnography is particularly suited to building theory when paired with an appropriate methodology, which is largely why I chose this method. Though difficult to employ, multisited ethnography allows unique insights into local and transnational processes that could not easily be discerned through a more traditional single-sited ethnography, as a multisited ethnography can facilitate comparative and relational understandings absent from single-sited studies. The methods section of the introduction laid the groundwork for the methodological approach used in this study, emphasizing that the choice of this particular method plays a central role in enabling the findings that I presented in later chapters.

Chapter 2 highlighted the complex and at times contradictory ways in which social ties in the workplace situate Haitian women within the nation. These social ties facilitated by paid labor at times include and at times exclude Haitian women from national belonging. Perhaps most intriguingly, chapter 2 presented examples of simultaneous inclusion and exclusion in workplace interactions. This chapter also explored how gender roles and class positions shifted for Haitian women of the first wave of migration under Duvalier, leaving middle- and upper-class Haitian women migrants in charge of housework for the first time in their lives in addition to entering the paid labor system in their new national contexts.

Chapter 3 uncovered the ways in which race and ethnicity are constructed and reconstructed in the workplace. Chapter 3 presented examples of how multisited ethnography is particularly applicable to the study of race and ethnicity and examined how race and ethnicity are constructed in the workplace transnationally, encouraging scholars of race theory to firmly plant theories in the specificities of local context in order to enable them to be adapted for the study of transnational processes.

Chapters 4 and 5 looked at the role of gender and class in labor for Haitian women in diaspora, illustrating the ways that gender and class situate Haitian women within their new national contexts. This examination contributes to an understanding of how gender and class intersect with cultural citizenship and belonging within the nation.

Chapter 6 draws together all the threads of the previous chapters, demonstrating how race, gender, and social ties in the workplace contribute to the concept of cultural citizenship, or national belonging, for Haitian women in the various nations in which they live and work. This chapter presented the origins and evolution of the term "cultural citizenship" and provided examples of Haitian women's daily workplace experiences that illustrate the concept of cultural citizenship in its complexities as it relates to race, migration, paid labor, and the nation. Scholars hotly debated conceptualizations of cultural citizenship in the late 1990s and early 2000s, but the term has largely fallen out of use since. Building on the work of other scholars of cultural citizenship, I argue for the utility of this term in understanding processes of national belonging, particularly in terms of paid labor.

Afterword

Since the conclusion of my fieldwork for this study in 2017, political instability and gang violence have increased dramatically in Haiti. Historically, periods of political instability and violence lead to increases in out-migration for those with the means to leave. The current gang violence in Haiti reportedly has internally displaced upwards of 350,000 people.[1] According to Evens Sanon and Dánica Coto at *PBS NewsHour*, "an estimated 200 gangs operate in Haiti, with the largest groups controlling up to 80 percent of the capital of Port-au-Prince."[2] Along with the proliferation of gang activity comes an increase in killings, kidnappings, and sexual violence against women and girls, putting Haitian women uniquely at risk.[3] Despite the increasingly dangerous situation in Haiti, the United States continues to deport migrants back to Haiti.

I have stayed in contact with many of the participants of this study and have anecdotally observed how they have adapted to new circumstances over time. Some have had children, others have changed jobs or moved to different countries altogether, and some have passed to join the ancestors. At least one participant moved from Montreal back to Haiti and was forced to leave for Miami because of the surge in violence in Haiti. These changes after the data collection reinforce the fact that this ethnographic study provides a snapshot in time but that these participants are not frozen in time. They lead full and vibrant lives that are constantly changing and evolving.

It has been a privilege to be invited into their lives to conduct this research, and I remain immeasurably grateful for their kindness and generosity. Their willingness to participate illustrates the Haitian spirit of unity in diaspora. By lifting me up in supporting my research, the sentiment was that they were lifting up the Haitian diaspora as a whole. Many of the participants in Montreal expressed an interest in my research results, though a number of them do not speak English. As a thank you and as a commitment to my participants, I wrote up an abbreviated version of my Montreal findings in French and distributed it to my participants so that they could see what they aided me in producing for my project. I plan to distribute my book as well, though it has been many years since I first conducted the research. Each of my participants is "building the nest" of Haiti and the Haitian diaspora in her own way, and I have attempted to continue that work here through my research.

I suspect that paid labor will continue to serve as a primary process that situates Haitian migrants in their new national contexts. While Haiti is in crisis, Haitian diasporic communities abroad continue to thrive. In some ways, paid labor gives Haitian migrants the resources necessary to support Haitian culture abroad. Paid labor also gives Haitian migrants the resources they need to attain varying degrees of cultural citizenship in their new homes. Haitian women migrants provide a specific case with some unique nuances, but this case also provides a framework for understanding processes of cultural citizenship and national belonging more generally.

Appendix A

Methodological Appendix

Expanded Methods

I lived in Boston while conducting my fieldwork from September to December 2011. Between 2011 and 2016, I made several preliminary trips to Montreal and Paris in order to establish networks and make contacts in communities there. I chose Montreal as the next site for my fieldwork because as another Western, North American site of migration yet in a different national context, it provides an interesting extension of my fieldwork in Boston, allowing for a study that extends beyond the United States to include another important place in the diaspora that is close in proximity yet culturally distinct from my Boston field site. I chose Paris for a completely different reason: given the colonial history between Haiti and France that has led the bourgeoisie in Haiti to identify with France in certain ways, I was interested in examining the experience of middle- and upper-class women in the metropole. I also thought it was generative to look at a site outside of North America to provide additional richness to the varied experiences of Haitian women in Western nations.[1]

In 2016–2017, I spent a year living and conducting fieldwork in each of my field sites. I lived full-time in Montreal, immersed in the Haitian community and conducting fieldwork from September 2016 to February 2017. I returned to Boston for the following three months to collect additional data to supplement my fieldwork in 2011, and lastly, I lived in Paris during June, July, and August of 2017 to conduct fieldwork with the Haitian diaspora there.

I had lived in both Paris and Boston previously but had little familiarity with Montreal prior to the start of this project. I needed more time there in order to understand Quebecois culture and therefore decided to spend the bulk of my time conducting fieldwork in 2016–2017 in Montreal. I made this decision knowing that this project may appear neater if I were to spend three to four months in each location during that year; however, the insights for this project have developed over an extended period of time, and to impose a false sense of compartmentalization contradicts the very purpose of this project. I aim to illustrate that the Haitian diaspora is fluid and not bound to any single location, making a traditional ethnography of space where a researcher lives or works in one neighborhood for several years unsuitable for this project. This transnational ethnography challenges traditional understandings of ethnography while drawing heavily from ethnographic methodology to shape my approach to this research.

Data Collection

I took detailed field notes on my observations in each of the cities, focusing on the particulars of the broader national culture and the ways in which Haitians forge their own sense of place and belonging. I initially focused my observations at Haitian cultural centers, music and dance events, and restaurants. As I continued, I conducted interviews in people's homes or places of employment when possible.

In addition to field notes and observations, I engaged in participant observation and conducted thirty-nine in-depth interviews that focused on challenges faced when emigrating from Haiti, experiences in finding housing and employment, and familial and other social networks in Haiti and in the country of residence. I used semistructured interview guides and digitally recorded interviews with consent from each participant. I coded each interview using Atlas.ti, qualitative data management software. The analysis process drew heavily from grounded theory in order to identify key themes such as racial and ethnic discrimination, gender roles, social ties, and cultural inclusion.[2]

Self-Reflexivity

I strongly value the importance of situating myself within the context of my research to better understand how my identity may have influenced interactions with participants and, in turn, my analysis of those interactions. My subject position as a second-generation Haitian granted me access to the population I sought to study. My status as an insider both allowed me to understand nuances of interactions that I observed and most likely led me to take certain phenomena for granted because they were so familiar, particularly in the context of my fieldwork in Boston, where I grew up as part of the Haitian community. Though I am not the subject of this research, because I am the daughter of a Haitian immigrant, this project is deeply personal. In negotiating access to research participants, I found myself negotiating my own sense of belonging within the Haitian diaspora on a personal level. Whether I was warmly welcomed or initially met with skepticism and reserve, the reactions of my research participants spoke not only to my role as a researcher but to my right to belong within the Haitian communities abroad.

I am American. I was born in Boston and my father is Jamaican, not Haitian. Growing up, we did not speak Haitian Kreyòl in the home. As a result of learning Kreyòl as an adult, my Kreyòl is slightly stilted and heavily accented, though Haitians are generally pleasantly surprised to discover that I took the initiative to learn my mother's native tongue.

I reflected on my identity as a researcher prior to engaging in fieldwork in an attempt to anticipate how various aspects of said identity may influence interactions with participants, though unexpected factors arose with regard to my identity when conducting interviews in Boston during the first stage of this research. I anticipated that my identity as a young Haitian American woman and my role in academia would serve as the primary factors influencing interactions with participants. I look at my identity as young, Haitian American, and a woman as intersecting and impossible to isolate. When participants meet me, they do not see only a woman, but a young Black woman. People often mistake me for being a decade younger than I am, giving me the appearance of one without much clout. I am sure that my gender and age put many participants at ease, making them more comfortable speaking to someone who could be their daughter or cousin than if I had been an older man. While those factors doubtless did play a role, I failed to take into account how my perceived class status as middle or upper class in Haitian society would influence the ease with which participants would interact with me.

My mother did, in fact, grow up in a middle-class family in Haiti, but since I was born in the United States and have never lived in Haiti, I did not anticipate that participants would read me as classed in terms of Haitian society. However, after conducting several interviews, I realized that my ease of access to this group of participants relied heavily on my class associations. This became clear when participants spoke to me about their class positions in Haiti or even class within the Haitian community in the United States. They spoke to me as though I would naturally understand the implications of their social class because I was one of them.

Skin color relates to perceptions of class in Haitian society to the point where there is a proverb that says, "Neg rich se milat, milat pov se neg," which in English means "A rich black person is a mulatto, a poor mulatto is black." Light skin is strongly associated with the middle and upper classes in Haiti. My light skin doubtless eased my entry into middle- and upper-class Haitian circles to complete fieldwork for this study.

Since I secured access to this initial population through existing social ties, I suspect that I would not have experienced as much success in securing access to participants outside of my family's social class. The social ties coupled with my perceived class status led many participants to exhibit a certain amount of cultural familiarity toward me without ever having met me, expressing an openness and eagerness to speak. However, I wonder if the fact that they clearly situated me in their class and social network prevented some participants from sharing details about their lives that they would have told someone they perceived as a total stranger. Despite the fact that I ensured confidentiality, some participants may have instinctively held back details for fear of how I as a peer would view them, or for fear of the information leaking back into their social circle.

Though I began my research through social ties in the Boston area, I found myself in Montreal and in Paris without any deep connection to the Haitian communities there. I found that my class status within Haitian society continued to play a role in securing my entry into certain circles and allowing me access to Haitians of a similar class. When meeting Haitians in Montreal and Paris, I always introduced myself as an American researcher but made sure to include that my mother is Haitian. Almost without fail, the first question out of Haitian participants' mouths was, "What is your family name?" My mother's maiden name is Arabic and somewhat obscure in Haiti because she is the descendent of a Syrian merchant somewhere on her father's side. Knowing that the question is about seeking some sort of recognition to determine whether or not I am properly Haitian, I frequently provided my grandmother's maiden name instead, since it is a very common name in Haiti and always sparks recognition. I knowingly sidestepped the at times tense relationship between Haitians of Syrian descent and the Haitian elite by leaning into my grandmother's family name and minimizing my allegiance with my grandfather's last name in order to position myself as an insider in the eyes of my participants, though on a personal level I also much more identify with my grandmother's lineage than my grandfather's. My grandfather was orphaned at a young age and raised by his Black Haitian godmother, so I don't know anything about his history other than what I can gather from his last name.

Doing this dance of claiming a Haitian identity and being challenged to verify that I am in fact Haitian and of the "right" class became second nature as I introduced myself to more and more Haitians in the field. While it made me uncomfortable to rely on my family's perceived class status to gain entry to the field, I also became acutely aware of the fact that very few people would be able to do this research in the same way. More than my role as a researcher, my identity as a Haitian woman was questioned in each interaction.

Appendix B

Overview of Interview Participants

This table contains descriptions of all the women I interviewed for this study, including those I do not mention by name in the manuscript. Though all of the interviews informed my analysis, callout quotes were chosen for how representative they were of my participants' experiences as a whole.

Location	Year of Interview	Pseudonym	Brief Bio
Boston	2011	Bernadette	A friendly and verbose woman, Bernadette was in her mid-sixties at the time of the interview. Bernadette married and moved to New York in the late 1960s to join her husband. Her husband was very controlling and did not want her to work, but she insisted on getting a job so that she would have some financial autonomy. Her first job was in a factory that produced cosmetics. She wanted to have her own money so that she could send money home to her family in Haiti. After five years of living in the States, Bernadette had two children and decided to leave her abusive husband and move to Boston with her children.
Boston	2011	Christine	A woman in her late fifties, Christine moved to New York in the late 1960s during early adolescence, migrating with her two sisters and their grandmother. They moved to the United States to join Christine's mother, who had migrated first and was working in New York to support herself, her children, and her mother, as well as extended family members back in Haiti. Christine started working as well a few years later after she moved to Boston with her family in 1971. Her first job was in a factory that produced wigs.
Boston	2011	Edwidge	At the time of the interview, Edwidge was a quick-witted woman in her mid-fifties who gave off a professional air and was impeccably dressed. While many of the other interviews took place in someone's home, Edwidge insisted on meeting in her office during the workday. After her parents moved to the United States for work in the late 1960s, Edwidge and her younger siblings joined her parents four years later, when she was sixteen years old. They initially migrated to New York, moving a year later when Edwidge's father found a job in Boston. Edwidge began working at the age of seventeen, after moving to Boston. Her first job was in a small factory, a job that she found through Haitian friends at her high school.

Location	Year of Interview	Pseudonym	Brief Bio
Boston	2017	Esther	At sixty-one years old, Esther had medium-light skin and natural hair pulled back in a severe low bun. She earned a degree in engineering but was unable to find work. While looking for a permanent position, she volunteered part-time for Fabienne's nonprofit doing office work.
Boston	2017	Fabienne	Fabienne was in her fifties but looked much younger. She had medium-dark skin and straightened shoulder-length hair, and she was always sharply dressed. She was the founder of a nonprofit in Boston aimed at helping Black girls. She was the mother of two adult children and widowed. She initially moved to Montreal from rural Haiti at age thirteen, and from Montreal to Boston at age seventeen. Her first job in Boston was working at a bridal shop where she was sexually harassed.
Boston	2011	Flore	An elegant woman at eighty years of age, Flore moved to Boston in the late 1950s to join her husband, who had moved first for work. Flore and her husband were one of the first Haitian families to move to Boston when they immigrated in the late 1950s. She proudly stated that she had been in the United States for fifty-three years at the time of the interview in 2011. Flore worked as a secretary in Haiti for a short time before getting married. After migrating, her time was mostly consumed with caring for her five children. When the youngest of her children started school, Flore began working in the public school system.
Boston	2011	Josephine	A woman in her early fifties when we spoke, Josephine and her family moved to Boston in 1975 when she was in early adolescence. She was able to find employment through her school's work-study program. At the age of eighteen, she married a kind man and moved to New York, where she continued working.

(continued)

Location	Year of Interview	Pseudonym	Brief Bio
Boston	2017	Josette	In her late thirties, Josette had medium-dark-brown skin and straightened black hair pulled back in a low ponytail. She worked for a nonprofit outside of Boston where she did not feel respected and valued. The mother of two young boys, Josette and her children moved to the States following the 2010 earthquake.
Boston	2011	Judeline	Before moving to the United States, Judeline was a young adult living with her parents in Haiti. Her niece, a woman many years her junior, had moved to Boston about five years before Judeline moved and was able to help her get settled when she arrived. Her niece helped her to find a place to live and helped her to find her first job. At the time of the interview, she said she worked at a conference center at a college, but I could not get her to reveal what type of work she did there. She was very reluctant to share about her life.
Boston	2011	Marie	A woman in her mid-fifties at the time of the interview, Marie moved to the United States in 1970 with her siblings when she was fifteen years old. They moved to join their mother, who had been working in Boston. Marie began working nights cleaning offices at the age of sixteen to pay her way through high school and to relieve some of the financial burden from her mother, who was working to feed and clothe all six of her children. Marie earned her college degree by attending night school while working full-time as a secretary.
Boston	2017	Marjorie	Marjorie was in her early sixties at the time of the interview. She was tall with medium-brown skin and short, dark-brown hair. She worked for a nonprofit providing social services for the Haitian community in Boston.
Boston	2011	Mona	In her early fifties at the time of the interview, Mona immigrated to Boston with her family when she was in her early teens. Though she did not know exactly what her parents' motivation to move was, she remembered that her father was

Location	Year of Interview	Pseudonym	Brief Bio
			involved in politics, and she suspected that they had to move for political reasons. Mona started her first job, cleaning offices at night in Boston, while attending high school when she was sixteen years old. When she moved to the United States, she had hoped to become a doctor. She sadly told me that due to finances she was unable to finish a postsecondary degree.
Boston	2011	Nadège	A tall, regal, light-skinned retiree who had lived in the United States for over forty years, Nadège was in her mid-sixties at the time of the interview. Her mother, who had been involved in politics in Haiti, fled to Boston and found a way for Nadège and her husband to join her about a year later. Upon arriving in Boston, Nadège found transitioning to life in the United States to be very challenging because she had always had domestic laborers to cook, clean, and raise children. She did not know how to cook or run a household, and she found herself with all of these new responsibilities and a newborn child to care for. She told me that as a woman she had to do everything because Haitian men don't do anything around the house.
Boston	2011	Patrice	In her late sixties at the time of the interview, Patrice moved to the United States in the 1970s as a young adult, after working as a secretary in Haiti. When she first moved to the United States, Patrice was working as a governess for a French family in Washington, D.C. After her one-year contract ended, Patrice moved to Boston to live with one of her sisters. She began working at a hotel, where she met her future husband. At the hotel she was in a supervisory role, made more money, and had the opportunity to travel for work. She later took classes to train as a medical secretary and had been in the same job for the past thirty-one years at the time of the interview. She loved her job, which allowed her to work as an interpreter for Haitian immigrants in the community in need of medical care.

(continued)

Location	Year of Interview	Pseudonym	Brief Bio
Boston	2017	Roseline	Roseline was in her late fifties to early sixties with short natural hair. Her hair was afro-like in texture and parted in the center. She was very funny and had a calm and relaxed demeanor. She taught English as a Second Language at a center in Boston.
Montreal	2017	Farah	Farah was a tall, dark-skinned woman with permed-straight, shoulder-length hair. She wore glasses and had a slight gap between her front teeth. She worked as an events manager for a company in Montreal. She also worked part-time as a wellness coach.
Montreal	2017	Gina	Gina was in her thirties. She was of average height and build with medium-brown skin and black, natural hair pulled back into a tight bun. She worked as a nurse.
Montreal	2017	Gladys	In her late sixties, Gladys was curvy and short in stature with straightened gray hair pulled back in a tight ponytail. She was a partially retired nurse who still frequently picked up shifts at an anglophone hospital. Additionally, she was very politically active in Quebec.
Montreal	2016	Guerda	In her late sixties, Guerda was small in stature with short gray hair and medium-brown skin. A retired nurse, she continued to work as a feminist activist in the Haitian community and was also active in Quebecois politics more broadly.
Montreal	2017	Karine	In her mid-thirties, Karine had light skin and curly natural hair that fell to her shoulders. She worked as a wellness coach helping clients to monitor their weight, meal plans, and exercise. In this capacity she ran fitness classes and trained others to work as wellness coaches as well. In addition to her work as a wellness coach, Karine was the founder of a dance group, taught dance almost every day, and performed as a professional dancer.
Montreal	2016	Martine	In her forties, Martine had very dark skin and short dark locs with highlights. She was very tall and had a big, warm smile. She lived and studied in Haiti through university. She worked in psychoeducation and was the mother of two little girls (ages five and eight).

Location	Year of Interview	Pseudonym	Brief Bio
Montreal	2016	Micheline	Micheline was in her sixties. She had medium-brown skin, short brown hair, and a lazy eye. She worked as a dance teacher, instructing her adult students in Haitian folkloric dance. She moved back and forth between Montreal and Haiti a few times in her adult life.
Montreal	2017	Mireille	Mireille was in her late sixties with light-brown skin and gray dreadlocks. She had an average build and a perpetually serious expression on her face. Mireille was an author.
Montreal	2017	Monique	Monique was in her late forties and had light-brown skin. She and her husband and son moved to Montreal after the 2010 earthquake. Though trained and working as a pediatrician in Haiti, her credentials were not recognized in Montreal. Instead, she worked in medical research.
Montreal	2017	Naomi	Naomi was a doctoral student in her early thirties. She had light skin and long, straight, brown hair. She was very involved with Maison d'Haïti.
Montreal	2017	Nathalie	At twenty-seven years old, Nathalie had very light skin and straightened hair. She was born and raised in Haiti, until pursuing university studies in Quebec. Her full-time job was as a social worker for the government, but she also taught and performed Haitian folkloric dance in the evenings and on the weekends. She had a sister in Montreal and a cousin in Washington, D.C.
Montreal	2017	Nicole	In her late twenties/early thirties, Nicole was heavyset with black, straightened hair. She was an experienced and advanced dancer recovering from an injury. She moved to Florida from Haiti in high school, and then to New York for a year before landing in Quebec. Her first job was working in the collections department for a phone company. Her job at the time of the interview was working for a pharmaceutical company.

(*continued*)

Location	Year of Interview	Pseudonym	Brief Bio
Montreal	2017	Rachelle	Rachelle was in her thirties with medium-brown skin and very short-cropped, red-dyed hair. She described herself as a militant social activist in the Haitian community. A close friend of Martine, Rachelle had recently finished grad school in psychology.
Montreal	2017	Sandra	Sandra was in her late thirties. She was a very small woman, both short and thin, with deep-brown skin and black hair kept in shoulder-length locs. Mother of three, Sandra was a psychologist and entrepreneur.
Montreal	2017	Simone	In her early seventies, Simone was a thin woman with dark-brown skin and straightened hair. She had a very warm and friendly manner. She talked *a lot* and spoke very quickly. She was a very successful, retired pediatrician.
Montreal	2017	Suzette	In her mid-fifties, Suzette had light skin and shoulder-length straightened hair. She worked in finance for the United Nations. She was a mother of two (ages thirty and nineteen) and had been married and divorced twice. She was struggling with bladder cancer.
Paris	2017	Beatrice	Beatrice was in her early fifties. She had dark skin and short, black, straightened hair that stood up in different directions. Her hair was unstraightened and graying around the edges near the roots. She dressed modestly in a green matching outfit with floral print. She moved to Paris with her husband and her resident permit did not allow her to work initially. She was a stay-at-home mother for years before working at a nursery.
Paris	2017	Cassandra	Cassandra was a middle-aged woman with light-brown skin and long, straightened, black hair that fell down her back. She smiled easily and often, revealing a single crooked bottom tooth. She was a lawyer and a first-time author who had recently published her first book.

Location	Year of Interview	Pseudonym	Brief Bio
Paris	2017	Johanne	Johanne was a thin middle-aged woman with very light skin and light-brown/hazel eyes. Her gray hair was wrapped around her head with a purple scarf, and she wore long, flowy white garments. When I complimented her on her clothing, she replied with a shrug, "Well, I'm an artist."
Paris	2017	Mirlande	Mirlande was a middle-aged woman with light-brown skin. She always dressed very modestly, even matronly, making her appear older than she was. Her hair was always pulled back in a tight bun at the nape of her neck and she wore a large, colorful 1980s-style headband. Born in Haiti, she first migrated to the United States, where she worked for a magazine in New York, and then to Paris, where she worked as a kindergarten teacher at a private school.
Paris	2017	Nadia	Nadia was a fifty-year-old woman with medium/dark-brown skin and shoulder-length straightened hair. In Haiti, she worked as a shopkeeper, just like her mother. She moved to Haiti with her ex-husband, who had proper documentation, though she did not. He resisted giving her access to papers for six years, and in that time it was very difficult to find work. She took care of the elderly, did housework, worked as a nanny, and assisted a disabled person. After getting her papers, she was unemployed because of an injury she sustained from an accident.
Paris	2017	Samantha	In her fifties, Samantha was an independent researcher and part-time lecturer. Diminutive in stature and thin, Samantha had a medium-brown complexion and wore her short brown hair with large curls and highlights.

(continued)

Location	Year of Interview	Pseudonym	Brief Bio
Paris	2017	Tamara	Tamara was a tall, middle-aged woman with very light skin dusted with freckles. She wore a long gray dress that clung to her curves, and her short, straight, black hair was messily styled atop her head. She worked for the United Nations in Paris after leaving Haiti, though her work with the United Nations took her all over the world.
Paris	2017	Wideline	In her early fifties, Wideline was tall and sturdy with medium-brown skin. At a Catholic event, she was flawlessly done up in a slinky green dress and makeup, and her hair was neatly braided in cornrows with blondish extensions. When I interviewed her at home, she was wearing an oversized African-print tunic as a muumuu and had unstyled short, black, straightened hair. She used to work in a nursery school before taking an administrative government role because of an injury.

Acknowledgments

This book would not have been possible without the strength, wisdom, and generosity of the Haitian women who participated in this study. I am thankful for each member of the Haitian diasporic community who welcomed me into their homes and places of work, graciously sharing their time, stories, and insights.

I am grateful for the guidance and input of so many along my journey to this point as a scholar. I began this project in 2011 at Simmons College, where I was nurtured and challenged as a young scholar. Jyoti Puri encouraged me to follow the trail of cultural citizenship in the earliest stages of this project, prompting me to pursue doctoral studies after completing my master's degree. She saw potential in this project when it was in its nascent stages, and her confidence in my ability to undertake this work inspired me to follow my passion.

Many faculty members at the University of California, Santa Barbara helped me to develop this project into the ethnographic work that shapes this book today. Victor Rios mentored me as an ethnographer, teaching me to become a more critical and reflexive researcher and providing helpful advice on navigating the academy. George Lipsitz supported this project from our first meeting, offering feedback on countless drafts and constantly helping me to develop more nuanced ways of framing my work. Claudine Michel offered scholarly guidance with warmth and kindness. She modeled how to be a Haitian scholar as well as a scholar of Haitian studies, always prioritizing the collective good. Additionally, classes with France Winddance Twine and Howard Winant allowed me to sharpen my analytical lens, challenging my work in productive ways.

Thank you to colleagues at Louisiana State University, particularly Stephen Finley in the program of African and African American Studies for his unwavering support and guidance as I pitched my manuscript to Rutgers University Press. The book publication process and my first role as a newly minted

PhD working as an assistant professor were a complete mystery to me as the first academic in my family. I cannot express how much I value the members of the African and African American Studies program at LSU for supporting me through those milestone moments. Thank you also to Heather O'Connell and Dana Berkowitz, who read drafts of chapters and articles related to this book and provided valuable feedback, and to my dear friend and colleague Chris Barrett for being one of my biggest cheerleaders. Your kindness and positive attitude have constantly buoyed my spirits.

My gratitude also goes to Anne Warfield Rawls at Bentley University for her feedback on the manuscript and staunch support of my work from the moment she met me. Her support allowed me to complete this manuscript through teaching, illness, and the challenges of starting at a new institution.

I give thanks to Maison d'Haïti in Montreal for their rich programming that helped me to get settled in the Haitian scholarly and activist community upon my arrival. I also thank the Centre for Oral History and Digital Storytelling at Concordia University in Montreal for welcoming me to view archives of interviews with Haitian women in Montreal, providing additional context and a more nuanced understanding of my own field work.

Thank you also to the Association of Haitian Women in Boston (AFAB) for your support of this project. I greatly admire your work and hope to collaborate with you further in the future.

Thank you to my editor at Rutgers University Press, Peter Mickulas, and the Inequality at Work Series editors, Enobong Hannah Branch and Adia Wingfield, for helping and encouraging me through this book project. Thank you for believing in this project when it was only a shadow of what it is today. I also thank the reviewers for their constructive feedback that allowed me to strengthen and develop this book in invaluable ways.

Lastly, but perhaps most importantly, my life partner Laura Powell has supported me every step of the way in this intellectual journey. Her love, patience and steady faith in me has seen me through the ups and downs of this process from start to finish. She has edited and copyedited so many drafts that she could probably recite this book from start to finish! I cannot thank her enough and I am certain that I would not have survived this journey without her in my corner. I am incredibly fortunate to have her in my life and to have her unwavering support.

Parts of this book were previously published as the following articles: Nikita Carney, "All Work Is Cultural Work," *Journal of Haitian Studies* 27, no. 1 (2021): 112–34; Nikita Carney, "Constructing Race and Ethnicity: 'It Has to Do with Where You Are,'" *Spatial Demography*, June 1, 2021, https://doi.org/10.1007/s40980-021-00087-6; Nikita Carney, "Race and Ethnicity across Borders: An Ethnographic Study of Haitian Women in Diaspora," *Issues in Race and Society* 11 (2023): 87–116.

Notes

Introduction

1   As clearly laid out in the work of Micheline Labelle (1987), the question of race in Haiti is complex and involves a racial hierarchy that does not easily map onto Western understandings of racial categories. I chose to focus on Blackness in Western terms because this work is predominantly targeted at Western audiences to learn about Haitian experiences. Micheline Labelle, *Idéologie de Couleur et Classes Sociales En Haïti* (Presses de l'Université de Montréal, 1987), http://classiques.uqac.ca/contemporains/labelle_micheline/ideologie_de_couleur_en_haiti/labelle_ideologie_couleur.pdf?

2   Thomas Faist, Margit Fauser, and Eveline Reisenauer, *Transnational Migration* (Polity, 2013).

3   Smith, Michael Peter, and Luis Eduardo Guarnizo, eds. *Transnationalism from Below*. Vol. 6. (Transaction Publishers, 1998); Michel Foucault, *Discipline and Punish: The Birth of the Prison* (Vintage Books, 1979); Ann Laura Stoler, *Carnal Knowledge and Imperial Power: Race and the Intimate in Colonial Rule* (University of California Press, 2010).

4   My project is not to compare and contrast the experiences of men and women. Rather, I seek to illuminate the ways in which the rich lived experiences of Haitian women should not be marginalized as a "special interest," because their unique experiences can push us to further develop our understanding of the general processes that govern citizenship and belonging. As a response to Rose Brewer's (2021) call for a Radical Black Feminist project, through this work I seek to address race, class, and gender within the context of the global political economy, centering the voices of Black women from the Global South. Rose M. Brewer, "The Radical Black Feminism Project: Rearticulating a Critical Sociology," in *Black Feminist Sociology: Perspectives and Praxis*, ed. Zakiya Luna and Whitney Pirtle (Routledge, 2021).

5   Louis Althusser, *For Marx*, vol. 2 (Verso, 1969).

6   Aihwa Ong, "Cultural Citizenship as Subject-Making," *Current Anthropology* 37, no. 5 (1996): 737–762.

7   Regine O. Jackson, ed., *Geographies of the Haitian Diaspora* (Routledge, 2011).

8 Nina Glick Schiller, Josh DeWind, Marie Lucie Brutus, Carolle Charles, Georges Fouron, and Antoine Thomas, "All in the Same Boat? Unity and Diversity in Haitian Organizing in New York," *Center for Migration Studies Special Issues* 7, no. 1 (1989): 167–184.

9 Pierrette Hondagneu-Sotelo, *Gender and U.S. Immigration: Contemporary Trends* (University of California Press, 2003), 13, Table of Contents, http://www.loc.gov /catdir/toc/fy038/2002043198.html.

10 Irene Bloemraad, Anna Korteweg, and Gökçe Yurdakul, "Citizenship and Immigration: Multiculturalism, Assimilation, and Challenges to the Nation-State," in *Annual Review of Sociology* 34, Annual Review of Sociology (Annual Reviews, 2008), 153–179; Thomas Faist, "Transnationalization in International Migration: Implications for the Study of Citizenship and Culture," *Ethnic and Racial Studies* 23, no. 2 (2000): 189–222; Toby Miller, *Cultural Citizenship: Cosmopolitanism, Consumerism, and Television in a Neoliberal Age* (Temple University Press, 2007).

11 Bloemraad, Korteweg, and Yurdakul, "Citizenship and Immigration"; Faist, "Transnationalization in International Migration"; Miller, *Cultural Citizenship.*

12 T. H. Marshall, *Class, Citizenship, and Social Development: Essays* (Anchor Books, 1965).

13 Bloemraad, Korteweg, and Yurdakul, "Citizenship and Immigration"; Nira Yuval-Davis, "Women, Citizenship and Difference," *Feminist Review* 57 (1997): 4–27.

14 Jean Beaman, "Citizenship as Cultural: Towards a Theory of Cultural Citizenship," *Sociology Compass* 10, no. 10 (2016): 849–857; Ong, "Cultural Citizenship as Subject-Making"; Renato Rosaldo, "Cultural Citizenship, Inequality, and Multiculturalism," in *Race, Identity, and Citizenship: A Reader*, ed. Rodolfo D. Torres, Louis F. Mirón, and Jonathan X. Inda (Blackwell, 1999), 253–261.

15 Nick Stevenson, "Cultural Citizenship in the 'Cultural' Society: A Cosmopolitan Approach," *Citizenship Studies* 7, no. 3 (2003): 331–348.

16 Ong, "Cultural Citizenship as Subject-Making."

17 Clifford Geertz, "Thick Description: Toward an Interpretive Theory of Culture," in *Readings in the Philosophy of Social Science*, ed. Michael Martin and Lee C. McIntyre (MIT Press, 1994), 213–231.

18 Jean Leca, "Questions on Citizenship," in *Dimensions of Radical Democracy: Pluralism, Citizenship, Community*, ed. Chantal Mouffe (Verso, 1992), 22.

19 Stuart Hall, "Race, Articulation, and Societies Structured in Dominance," in *Black British Cultural Studies: A Reader*, ed. Houston A. Baker Jr., Manthia Diawara, and Ruth H. Lindesborg (University of Chicago Press, 1996), 16–60; Stevenson, "Cultural Citizenship."

20 Among other works, Rosaldo, "Cultural Citizenship, Inequality, and Multiculturalism"; Ong, "Cultural Citizenship as Subject-Making."

21 Ong, "Cultural Citizenship as Subject-Making."

22 Devon W. Carbado, "Racial Naturalization," *American Quarterly* 57, no. 3 (2005): 633–658.

23 Carbado, "Racial Naturalization."

24 Stevenson, "Cultural Citizenship."

25 Miller, *Cultural Citizenship.*

26 Scholars who have greatly contributed to this field included Renato Rosaldo, "Cultural Citizenship and Educational Democracy," *Cultural Anthropology* 9,

no. 3 (1994): 402–411; Cati Coe, *The New American Servitude: Political Belonging Among African Immigrant Home Care Workers* (New York University Press, 2019); Alyshia Gálvez, "Immigrant Citizenship: Neoliberalism, Immobility and the Vernacular Meanings of Citizenship," *Identities* 20, no. 6 (2013): 720–737; Juan Flores, "'Que Assimilated, Brother, Yo Soy Asimilao': The Structuring of Puerto Rican Identity in the US," *The Journal of Ethnic Studies* 13, no. 3 (1985): 1–16; Adelaida Del Castillo, "Illegal Status and Social Citizenship: Thoughts on Mexican Immigrants in a Postnational World," in *Women and Migration in the US-Mexico Borderlands: A Reader*, ed. Denise A. Segura and Patricia Zavella (Duke University Press, 2007); and Orly Clerge, *The New Noir: Race, Identity, and Diaspora in Black Suburbia* (University of California Press, 2019).

27   Rosaldo, "Cultural Citizenship and Educational Democracy."

28   Coe, *New American Servitude*, 8.

29   Coe, *New American Servitude*, 8.

30   Coe, *New American Servitude*, 7.

31   Gálvez, "Immigrant Citizenship."

32   Since legal migration status is such a sensitive, and potentially dangerous, topic to discuss, I explicitly chose not to ask participants about their legal migration status.

33   Juan Flores, "'Que Assimilated, Brother, Yo Soy Asimilao': The Structuring of Puerto Rican Identity in the US," *The Journal of Ethnic Studies* 13, no. 3 (1985): 12.

34   Del Castillo, "Illegal Status and Social Citizenship."

35   Del Castillo, "Illegal Status and Social Citizenship."

36   Clerge, *New Noir*, 6.

37   Clerge, *New Noir*, 6.

38   Rose M. Brewer, "Theorizing Race, Class and Gender: The New Scholarship of Black Feminist Intellectuals and Black Women's Labor," *Race, Gender & Class* 6, no. 2 (1999): 29–47; Aihwa Ong, *Spirits of Resistance and Capitalist Discipline: Factory Women in Malaysia* (State University of New York Press, 2010).

39   Margaret Benston, "The Political Economy of Women's Liberation," *Monthly Review* 41, no. 7 (1989): 31–44.

40   Hondagneu-Sotelo, *Gender and U.S. Immigration*, 11.

41   Nancy Foner, "Gender and Migration: West Indians in Comparative Perspective," *International Migration* 47, no. 1 (2009): 3–29.

42   Tamara Mose Brown, *Raising Brooklyn: Nannies, Childcare, and Caribbeans Creating Community* (New York University Press, 2011).

43   For more reading on gender and migration studies, see Richard D. Alba and Nancy Foner, "Comparing Immigrant Integration in North America and Western Europe: How Much Do the Grand Narratives Tell Us?," *International Migration Review* 48 (Fall 2014): S263–S291; Tanja Bastia, "Intersectionality, Migration and Development," *Progress in Development Studies* 14, no. 3 (2014): 237–248; Sara R. Curran, Steven Shafer, Katharine M. Donato, and Feliz Garip, "Mapping Gender and Migration in Sociological Scholarship: Is It Segregation or Integration?," *International Migration Review* 40, no. 1 (2006): 199–223; Katharine M. Donato, Donna Gabaccia, Jennifer Holdaway, Martin Manalansan, and Patricia R. Pessar, "A Glass Half Full? Gender in Migration Studies," *International Migration Review* 40, no. 1 (2006): 3–26; Hondagneu-Sotelo, *Gender and U.S. Immigration*; Helma Lutz, "Gender in the Migratory Process," *Journal of Ethnic & Migration Studies* 36, no. 10 (2010): 1647–1663; Sarah J. Mahler and Patricia R. Pessar, "Gender Matters: Ethnographers Bring Gender

from the Periphery toward the Core of Migration Studies," *International Migration Review* 40, no. 1 (2006): 27–63; Patricia R. Pessar, "Engendering Migration Studies: The Case of New Immigrants in the United States," in *Gender and U.S. Immigration: Contemporary Trends* (University of California Press, 2003), 20–42, http://www.jstor.org/stable/10.1525/j.ctt1pntog.5.

44 Curran et al., "Mapping Gender and Migration"; Donato et al., "Glass Half Full?"
45 Gioconda Herrera, "Gender and International Migration: Contributions and Cross-Fertilizations," *Annual Review of Sociology* 39 (2013): 471.
46 Bastia, "Intersectionality, Migration and Development," 237.
47 Bastia, "Intersectionality, Migration and Development."
48 Notable exceptions include the works of Carolle Charles, "Gender and Politics in Contemporary Haiti: The Duvalierist State, Transnationalism, and the Emergence of a New Feminism (1980–1990)," *Feminist Studies* 21, no. 1 (1995): 135–164; Elizabeth McAlister, "Sacred Stories from the Haitian Diaspora: A Collective Biography of Seven Vodou Priestesses in New York City," *Journal of Caribbean Studies* 9, no. 1 & 2 (1993): 10–27; Georges Fouron and Nina Glick Schiller, "All in the Family: Gender, Transnational Migration, and the Nation-State," *Identities: Global Studies in Culture and Power* 7, no. 4 (2001) : 539–582; and Jennifer Shoaff, "Haitian Migrant Women, Dominican Pepeceras, and the Power Geographies of Transnational Markets," in *Transatlantic Feminisms: Women and Gender Studies in Africa and the Diaspora*, ed. Cheryl R. Rodriguez et al. (Lexington Books, 2015).
49 Patricia R. Pessar and Sarah J. Mahler, "Transnational Migration: Bringing Gender In," *International Migration Review* 37, no. 3 (2003): 815.
50 Pessar and Mahler, "Transnational Migration," 818.
51 Bloemraad, Korteweg, and Yurdakul, "Citizenship and Immigration"; Faist, "Transnationalization in International Migration"; Faist, Fauser, and Reisenauer, *Transnational Migration*; Herrera, "Gender and International Migration"; José Itzigsohn, "Immigration and the Boundaries of Citizenship: The Institutions of Immigrants' Political Transnationalism," *International Migration Review* 34, no. 4 (2000): 1126–1154; Peggy Levitt and B. Nadya Jaworsky, "Transnational Migration Studies: Past Developments and Future Trends," *Annual Review of Sociology* 33 (2007): 129–156; Aihwa Ong, *Flexible Citizenship: The Cultural Logics of Transnationality* (Duke University Press, 1999); Pessar and Mahler, "Transnational Migration"; Schiller and Fouron, "Terrains of Blood and Nation."
52 Faist, "Transnationalization in International Migration"; Faist, Fauser, and Reisenauer, *Transnational Migration*.
53 Mary C. Waters, *Black Identities: West Indian Immigrant Dreams and American Realities* (Russell Sage Foundation; Harvard University Press, 1999).
54 Bloemraad, Korteweg, and Yurdakul, "Citizenship and Immigration," 154.
55 Linda G. Basch, Nina Glick Schiller, and Cristina Szanton Blanc, *Nations Unbound: Transnational Projects, Postcolonial Predicaments, and Deterritorialized Nation-States* (Gordon and Breach, 2005); Louis Herns Marcelin, "Identity, Power, and Socioracial Hierarchies Among Haitian Immigrants in Florida," in *Neither Enemies nor Friends: Latinos, Blacks, Afro- Latinos*, ed. Anani Dzidzienyo and Suzanne Oboler (Palgrave Macmillan, 2005); Manuel Orozco and Elisabeth Burgess, "A Commitment Amidst Shared Hardship: Haitian Transnational Migrants and Remittances," *Journal of Black Studies* 42, no. 2 (2011): 225–246.
56 Basch, Schiller, and Szanton Blanc, *Nations Unbound*.

57 Georges Fouron and Nina Glick Schiller, "All in the Family: Gender, Transna-
    tional Migration, and the Nation-State," *Identities: Global Studies in Culture and
    Power* 7, no. 4 (2001): 539–582.
58 Fouron and Schiller, "All in the Family," 3.
59 Orozco and Burgess, "Commitment Amidst Shared Hardship."
60 Rhacel Salazar Parreñas, *Servants of Globalization: Migration and Domestic Work*
    (Stanford University Press, 2015); Ernesto Castañeda, *A Place to Call Home:
    Immigrant Exclusion and Urban Belonging in New York, Paris, and Barcelona*
    (Stanford University Press, 2018).
61 Nikita Carney, "Multi-Sited Ethnography: Opportunities for the Study of Race,"
    Sociology Compass 11, no. 9 (2017): 2.
62 Carney, "Multi-Sited Ethnography," 4.
63 Karen McCarthy Brown and Claudine Michel, *Mama Lola: A Vodou Priestess in
    Brooklyn*, vol. 4 (University of California Press, 2010); Nina Glick Schiller and
    Georges Eugene Fouron, *Georges Woke up Laughing: Long-Distance Nationalism
    and the Search for Home* (Duke University Press, 2001); Clerge, *New Noir*.
64 Brown and Michel, *Mama Lola*.
65 As stated by Karen McCarthy Brown in *Mama Lola*, "Haitian Vodou is not only
    one of the most misunderstood religions in the world; it is also one of the most
    maligned" (xli). My mother likely encountered racist and xenophobic anti-Vodou
    rhetoric upon arriving in Boston, solidifying her desire to distance herself from
    Vodou in favor of assimilation.

Chapter 1   Haiti in a Global Context

1   Joan Dayan, *Haiti, History, and Gods* (University of California Press, 1995).
2   Michel-Rolph Trouillot, *Silencing the Past: Power and the Production of History*
    (Beacon, 1995).
3   Hans Schmidt, *The United States Occupation of Haiti, 1915–1934* (Rutgers
    University Press, 1995).
4   Andrew Levin, "Civil Society and Democratization in Haiti," *Emory Interna-
    tional Law Review* 9, no. 389 (1995).
5   Erica Caple James, *Democratic Insecurities: Violence, Trauma, and Intervention in
    Haiti* (University of California Press, 2010).
6   Mark Schuller, "Participation, More than Add Women and Stir? A Comparative
    Case Analysis in Post-Coup Haiti," *Caribbean Review of Gender Studies* 2 (2008):
    2.
7   Linda G. Basch, Nina Glick Schiller, and Cristina Szanton Blanc, *Nations
    Unbound: Transnational Projects, Postcolonial Predicaments, and Deterritorialized
    Nation-States* (Gordon and Breach, 2005).
8   Basch, Schiller, and Szanton Blanc, *Nations Unbound*; Claude Delachet-Guillon,
    La Communauté Haïtienne En Ile-de-France (Editions L'Harmattan, 1996).
9   Renaud Bernardin, "Le Canada, Le Québec et Haiti," *Le Devoir*, November 7,
    1974 ; Marilynn S. Johnson, *The New Bostonians* (University of Massachusetts
    Press, 2015), http://www.jstor.org.libezp.lib.lsu.edu/stable/j.ctt1cx3tdr.
10 Basch, Schiller, and Szanton Blanc, *Nations Unbound*.
11 J. P. Linstroth, Alison Hall, Mamyrah A. Douge-Prosper, and Patrick T. Hiller,
    "Conflicting Ambivalence of Haitian Identity-Making in South Florida," *Forum:
    Qualitative Social Research* 10, no. 3 (2009): 1–37.

12 Michel S. Laguerre, *Diasporic Citizenship: Haitian Americans in Transnational America* (St. Martin's, 1998).

13 Laguerre, *Diasporic Citizenship*.

14 Christian Joppke, "Multiculturalism and Immigration: A Comparison of the United States, Germany, and Great Britain," *Theory and Society* 25, no. 4 (1996): 449–500; Tariq Modood and Pnina Werbner, *The Politics of Multiculturalism in the New Europe: Racism, Identity, and Community* (Zed Books, 1997).

15 Basch, Schiller, and Szanton Blanc, *Nations Unbound*.

16 Steven Ruggles, Sarah Flood, Ronald Goeken, Josiah Grover, Erin Meyer, Jose Pacas, and Matthew Sobek, "IPUMS USA: Version 10.0 [Dataset]" (IPUMS, 2020), https://doi.org/10.18128/D010.V10.0.

17 Thomas M. Menino, "Imagine All the People: Haitian Immigrants in Boston," New Bostonian Series (City of Boston, June 2009).

18 Angela B. Buchanan, Nora G. Albert, and Daniel Beaulieu, "The Population with Haitian Ancestry in the United States: 2009," *American Community Survey Briefs* (U.S. Census Bureau, October 2010); U.S. Census Bureau, "American Community Survey," 2021, https://data.census.gov/table?q=haitians+demographics&t=581&tid=ACSSPP1Y2021.S0201.

19 Jim Vrabel, *A People's History of the New Boston* (University of Massachusetts Press, 2014), http://www.jstor.org/stable/j.ctt5vk3fs.

20 Johnson, *New Bostonians*.

21 Johnson, *New Bostonians*.

22 Johnson, *New Bostonians*, 2.

23 Johnson, *New Bostonians*.

24 Brahim Boudarbat, Maude Boulet, and others, "Immigration Au Québec: Politiques et Intégration Au Marché Du Travail" (CIRANO, 2010); Carol-Anne Gauthier, "Obstacles to Socioeconomic Integration of Highly-Skilled Immigrant Women: Lessons from Quebec Interculturalism and Implications for Diversity Management," ed. Charlotte Holgersson, Irene Ryan, and Inge Bleijenbergh, *Equality, Diversity and Inclusion: An International Journal* 35, no. 1 (2016): 17–30, https://doi.org/10.1108/EDI-03-2014-0022; Cory Blad and Philippe Couton, "The Rise of an Intercultural Nation: Immigration, Diversity and Nationhood in Quebec," *Journal of Ethnic & Migration Studies* 35, no. 4 (2009): 645–667, https://doi.org/10.1080/13691830902765277.

25 Blad and Couton, "Rise of an Intercultural Nation,"646–647.

26 Micheline Labelle and François Rocher, "Immigration, Integration and Citizenship Policies in Canada and Quebec," in *Immigration and Self-Government of Minority Nations*, ed. Ricard Zapata-Barrero (Peter Lang, 2009), 57–86; Blad and Couton, "Rise of an Intercultural Nation," 652.

27 Gauthier, "Obstacles to Socioeconomic Integration," 22.

28 Most of these demographic changes have taken place in urban spaces in Quebec, particularly in Montreal.

29 Blad and Couton, "Rise of an Intercultural Nation," 660.

30 Blad and Couton, "Rise of an Intercultural Nation," 647.

31 Sébastien Arcand, Annick Lenoir-Achdjian, and Denise Helly, "Insertion Professionnelle d'immigrants Récents et Réseaux Sociaux: Le Cas de Maghrébins à Montréal et Sherbrooke," *The Canadian Journal of Sociology / Cahiers Canadiens de Sociologie* 34, no. 2 (2009): 373–402; Gauthier, "Obstacles to Socioeconomic Integration"; Jeffrey G. Reitz, "Immigrant Employment Success in Canada, Part I:

Individual and Contextual Causes," *Journal of International Migration and Integration / Revue de l'integration et de La Migration Internationale* 8, no. 1 (2007): 11–36, https://doi.org/10.1007/s12134-007-0001-4; Jeffrey G. Reitz, "Immigrant Employment Success in Canada, Part II: Understanding the Decline," *Journal of International Migration and Integration / Revue de l'integration et de La Migration Internationale* 8, no. 1 (2007): 37–62, https://doi.org/10.1007/s12134-007-0002-3.

32 Gauthier, "Obstacles to Socioeconomic Integration."

33 Blad and Couton, "Rise of an Intercultural Nation"; Labelle and Rocher, "Immigration, Integration."

34 Blad and Couton, "Rise of an Intercultural Nation."

35 Blad and Couton, "Rise of an Intercultural Nation," 659.

36 Chris Kostov, "Canada-Quebec Immigration Agreements (1971–1991) and Their Impact on Federalism," *American Review of Canadian Studies* 38, no. 1 (2008): 91–103, https://doi.org/10.1080/02722010809481822.

37 Sean Mills, "Quebec, Haiti, and the Deportation Crisis of 1974," *The Canadian Historical Review* 94, no. 3 (2013): 405–435; Scooter Pegram, "Being Ourselves: Immigrant Culture and Self-Identification Among Young Haitians in Montréal," *Ethnic Studies Review* 28 (2005): 1–20.

38 Herard Jadotte, "Haitian Immigration to Quebec," *Journal of Black Studies* 7, no. 4 (1977): 485–500.

39 Government of Canada, Statistics Canada, "Census Profile, 2016 Census—Montréal, Ville [Census Subdivision], Quebec and Quebec [Province]," February 8, 2017, https://www12.statcan.gc.ca/census-recensement/2016/dp-pd/prof/details/page.cfm?Lang=E&Geo1=CSD&Code1=2466023&Geo2=PR&Code2=24&SearchText=Montreal&SearchType=Begins&SearchPR=01&B1=Ethnic%20origin&TABID=1&type=0.

40 Micheline Labelle, Serge Larose, and Victor Piché, "Émigration et immigration: Les Haïtiens au Québec," *Sociologie et sociétés* 15, no. 2 (1983): 73–88, https://doi.org/10.7202/001394ar.

41 Joan Wallach Scott, *The Politics of the Veil* (Princeton University Press, 2009).

42 Roger Cohen, "Muslim Students' Robes Are Latest Fault Line for French Identity," *New York Times*, September 15, 2023, sec. World, https://www.nytimes.com/2023/09/15/world/europe/france-abaya-ban-attal.html; Iannis Roder, "Abaya Ban in French Schools: 'Wearing the Abaya Is a Political Gesture,'" *Le Monde*, September 9, 2023, https://www.lemonde.fr/en/opinion/article/2023/09/09/france-s-abaya-ban-wearing-the-abaya-is-a-political-gesture_6131329_23.html.

43 Adrian Favell, *Philosophies of Integration: Immigration and the Idea of Citizenship in France and Britain* (Springer, 2016), 3.

44 Favell, *Philosophies of Integration*, 3.

45 Favell, *Philosophies of Integration*, 70.

46 Favell, *Philosophies of Integration*, 73.

47 Favell, *Philosophies of Integration*, 8.

48 Favell, *Philosophies of Integration*, 9–10.

49 Jane Freedman, *Immigration and Insecurity in France* (Routledge, 2017), https://doi.org/10.4324/9781315252582.

50 Alec G. Hargreaves, *Multi-Ethnic France: Immigration, Politics, Culture and Society*, 2nd ed. (Routledge, 2007), 3. https://doi.org/10.4324/9780203962794.

51   Etienne Balibar, "Racism as Universalism," *New Political Science* 8, no. 1–2 (1989): 9–22.

52   Lisa Lowe, *Immigrant Acts: On Asian American Cultural Politics* (Duke University Press, 1996).

53   Jean Beaman, *Citizen Outsider: Children of North African Immigrants in France* (University of California Press, 2017), 19.

54   Beaman, *Citizen Outsider*, 47.

55   Beaman, *Citizen Outsider*, 49.

56   David Voas and Fenella Fleischmann, "Islam Moves West: Religious Change in the First and Second Generations," *Annual Review of Sociology* 38, no. 1 (2012): 525–545; Beaman, *Citizen Outsider*; Erik Bleich, "Muslims and the State in the Post-9/11 West: Introduction," *Journal of Ethnic and Migration Studies* 35, no. 3 (2009): 353–360; Erik Bleich, "On Democratic Integration and Free Speech: Response to Tariq Modood and Randall Hansen," *International Migration* 44, no. 5 (2006): 17–22.

57   Hargreaves, *Multi-Ethnic France*, 31.

58   Hargreaves, *Multi-Ethnic France*.

59   "Étrangers—Immigrés En 2016" (L'Institut national de la statistique et des études économiques, 2019), https://www.insee.fr/fr/statistiques/4177162?sommaire =4177618&geo=FE-1.

60   Félix F. Germain, "Caribbean Women in Postwar France, 1946–1974," in *Decolonizing the Republic*, African and Caribbean Migrants in Postwar Paris, 1946–1974 (Michigan State University Press, 2016), 92, http://www.jstor.org /stable/10.14321/j.ctt1bkm6rf.10.

Chapter 2   Social Ties and Complex Inclusion in the Nation

1   Nathalie's experience of working within an ethnic enclave and then using skills acquired there to assimilate into the larger national frame is representative of a few of the women I spoke with in Montreal.

2   See Louise Lamphere, Alex Stepick, and Guillermo J. Grenier, *Newcomers in the Workplace: Immigrants and the Restructuring of the U.S. Economy* (Temple University Press, 1994).

3   Aihwa Ong, *Flexible Citizenship: The Cultural Logics of Transnationality* (Duke University Press, 1999).

4   Ong, *Flexible Citizenship*, 88.

5   Ong, *Flexible Citizenship*, 112.

6   Ong, *Flexible Citizenship*, 113.

7   Though outside the scope of this project, Haitian immigrants in Paris from the south of Haiti, typically of a lower socioeconomic class, experienced a different migration flow and experience within established communities in the suburbs of Paris. I suspect that Haitian immigrants from impoverished backgrounds experience national belonging through work differently due to their class position prior to migration.

8   See Annie Hikido's work "Entrepreneurship in South African Township Tourism: The Impact of Interracial Social Capital," *Ethnic and Racial Studies* 41, no. 14 (2018): 2580–2598, on bed and breakfasts in South Africa.

9   Nancy Foner, "Benefits and Burdens: Immigrant Women and Work in New York City," *Gender Issues* 16, no. 4 (1998): 20.

10 Ong, *Flexible Citizenship*.
11 Lalaie Ameeriar, *Downwardly Global: Women, Work, and Citizenship in the Pakistani Diaspora* (Duke University Press, 2017).
12 See Jean Beaman, *Citizen Outsider: Children of North African Immigrants in France* (University of California Press, 2017).
13 Juan Flores, "'Que Assimilated, Brother, Yo Soy Asimilao': The Structuring of Puerto Rican Identity in the US," *The Journal of Ethnic Studies* 13, no. 3 (1985): 11.
14 Aihwa Ong, *Spirits of Resistance and Capitalist Discipline: Factory Women in Malaysia* (State University of New York Press, 2010).
15 Ong, *Spirits of Resistance*, 201.
16 Mary C. Waters, *Black Identities: West Indian Immigrant Dreams and American Realities* (Russell Sage Foundation; Harvard University Press, 1999).

Chapter 3 Gendered Race and Ethnicity Across Borders

1 Though not explicitly the focus of this chapter, the experiences of Haitian women in diaspora shape their identities with regard to Haiti as well as to the United States, Canada, and France.
2 The "afterlife of slavery" is in quotations here to indicate that the effects of slavery continue to shape daily life for the descendants of slaves through Reconstruction, the Civil Rights Movement, and today with the Black Lives Matter movement.
3 Linda G. Basch, Nina Glick Schiller, and Cristina Szanton Blanc, *Nations Unbound: Transnational Projects, Postcolonial Predicaments, and Deterritorialized Nation-States* (Gordon and Breach, 2005); Mary C. Waters, *Black Identities: West Indian Immigrant Dreams and American Realities* (Russell Sage Foundation; Harvard University Press, 1999).
4 Micheline Labelle, *Idéologie de Couleur et Classes Sociales En Haïti* (Presses de l'Université de Montréal Montreal, 1987), http://classiques.uqac.ca/contemporains/labelle_micheline/ideologie_de_couleur_en_haiti/labelle_ideologie_couleur.pdf?
5 Waters, *Black Identities*, 31.
6 François Pierre-Louis, "Haitian Immigrants and the Greater Caribbean Community of New York City: Challenges and Opportunities," *Memorias: Revista Digital de Historia y Arqueología Desde El Caribe* 10, no. 21 (2013): 22–40.
7 Ronald P. Formisano, *Boston Against Busing: Race, Class, and Ethnicity in the 1960s and 1970s* (University of North Carolina Press, 2004); Alan Lupo, *Liberty's Chosen Home: The Politics of Violence in Boston* (Beacon, 1988).
8 Basch, Schiller, and Szanton Blanc, *Nations Unbound*; Nikita Carney, "Constructing Race and Ethnicity: 'It Has to Do with Where You Are,'" *Spatial Demography*, June 1, 2021, https://doi.org/10.1007/s40980-021-00087-6; Louis Herns Marcelin, "Identity, Power, and Sociocracial Hierarchies Among Haitian Immigrants in Florida," in *Neither Enemies nor Friends: Latinos, Blacks, Afro-Latinos*, ed. Anani Dzidzienyo and Suzanne Oboler (Palgrave Macmillan, 2005); Waters, *Black Identities*.
9 Oscar Handlin, *Boston's Immigrants, 1790–1880: A Study in Acculturation* (Harvard University Press, 1991); Thomas H. O'Connor, *The Boston Irish: A Political History* (Northeastern University Press, 1995); John F. Stack Jr., *International Conflict in an American City: Boston's Irish, Italians, and Jews, 1935–1944* (Greenwood, 1979).

10 S. Charusheela, "Empowering Work? Bargaining Models Reconsidered," in *Toward a Feminist Philosophy of Economics*, ed. Drucilla K. Barker and Edith Kuiper (Routledge, 2003), 287–300; Marlene Kim, "Race and Ethnicity in the Workplace," in *Handbook of Research on Gender and Economic Life*, ed. Deborah M. Figart and Tonia L. Warnecke, (Edward Elgar, 2013), 218–235.

11 Charusheela, "Empowering Work?," 298.

12 Claude Delachet-Guillon, *La Communauté Haïtienne En Ile-de-France* (Editions L'Harmattan, 1996); Waters, *Black Identities*.

13 Marilynn S. Johnson, *The New Bostonians: How Immigrants Have Transformed the Metro Area Since the 1960s* (University of Massachusetts Press, 2015), http://www.jstor.org.libezp.lib.lsu.edu/stable/j.ctt1cx3tdr.

14 Mary C. Waters, "West Indians and African Americans at Work: Structural Differences and Cultural Stereotypes," in *Immigration and Opportunity: Race, Ethnicity, and Employment in the United States*, ed. Stephanie Bell-Rose and Frank D. Bean (Russell Sage Foundation, 2003), 194, http://muse.jhu.edu/book/42175.

15 Waters, "West Indians and African Americans," 195.

16 Rose M. Brewer, "Theorizing Race, Class and Gender: The New Scholarship of Black Feminist Intellectuals and Black Women's Labor," *Race, Gender & Class* 6, no. 2 (1999): 29–47.

17 Jean Beaman, *Citizen Outsider: Children of North African Immigrants in France* (University of California Press, 2017).

18 Brewer, "Theorizing Race, Class and Gender"; Manning Marable, *How Capitalism Underdeveloped Black America: Problems in Race, Political Economy, and Society* (Haymarket Books, 2015).

19 Brewer, "Theorizing Race, Class and Gender"; Kim, "Race and Ethnicity."

20 See Adia Harvey Wingfield, *Flatlining: Race, Work, and Health Care in the New Economy* (University of California Press, 2019).

21 Frantz Fanon, *Black Skin, White Masks* (Grove, 1952); Paul Gilroy, *The Black Atlantic: Modernity and Double Consciousness* (Harvard University Press, 1993); M. Jacqui Alexander, *Pedagogies of Crossing: Meditations on Feminism, Sexual Politics, Memory, and the Sacred* (Duke University Press, 2005).

Chapter 4   Gender Roles and Work, In and Out of the Home

1 On gender and labor: Rose M. Brewer, "Theorizing Race, Class and Gender: The New Scholarship of Black Feminist Intellectuals and Black Women's Labor," *Race, Gender & Class* 6, no. 2 (1999): 29–47; S. Charusheela, "Empowering Work? Bargaining Models Reconsidered," in *Toward a Feminist Philosophy of Economics*, ed. Drucilla K. Barker and Edith Kuiper (Routledge, 2003), 287–300.

On the relationship between gender and migration: Patricia R. Pessar and Sarah J. Mahler, "Transnational Migration: Bringing Gender In," *International Migration Review* 37, no. 3 (2003): 812–846; also see Helma Lutz, "Gender in the Migratory Process," *Journal of Ethnic & Migration Studies* 36, no. 10 (2010): 1647–1663; Nancy Foner, "Benefits and Burdens: Immigrant Women and Work in New York City," *Gender Issues* 16 (September 1, 1998): 5–24, https://doi.org/10.1007/s12147-998-0008-y; Nancy Foner, "Gender and Migration: West Indians in Comparative Perspective," *International Migration* 47, no. 1 (2009): 3–29; and

Tanja Bastia, "Intersectionality, Migration and Development," *Progress in Development Studies* 14, no. 3 (2014): 237–248.

    On gender, work and migration: See scholars such as Rhacel Salazar Parreñas, *Servants of Globalization: Migration and Domestic Work* (Stanford University Press, 2015); Megha Amrith and Nina Sahraoui, *Gender, Work and Migration: Agency in Gendered Labour Settings* (Routledge, 2018).

2 Linda Basch, Nina Glick Schiller, and Christina Szanton Blanc, *Nations Unbound: Transnational Projects, Postcolonial Predicaments, and Deterritorialized Nation-States* (Routledge, 2005); Blandine Mollard and Sanober Umar, "Gender, Migration and Deskilling: A Broad Review of the Literature," in *Crushed Hopes: Underemployment and Deskilling Among Skilled Migrant Women* (International Organization for Migration, 2013), 9–36.

3 Parreñas, *Servants of Globalization.*

4 Maxine L. Margolis, "From Mistress to Servant: Downward Mobility Among Brazilian Immigrants in New York City," *Urban Anthropology and Studies of Cultural Systems and World Economic Development* 19, no. 3 (1990): 215–231.

5 Micheline Labelle, *Idéologie de Couleur et Classes Sociales En Haïti* (Presses de l'Université de Montréal Montreal, 1987), http://classiques.uqac.ca/contemporains /labelle_micheline/ideologie_de_couleur_en_haiti/labelle_ideologie_couleur.pdf?

6 Though colorism certainly exists in the United States, structures of racism still marginalize and oppress even light-skinned Haitian women. See, for colorism in the United States, Margaret Hunter, "The Persistent Problem of Colorism: Skin Tone, Status, and Inequality," *Sociology Compass* 1, no. 1 (2007): 237–254, https://doi.org/10.1111/j.1751-9020.2007.00006.x.

7 Brewer, "Theorizing Race, Class and Gender."

8 Kristyn Frank and Feng Hou, "Source-Country Gender Roles and the Division of Labor Within Immigrant Families," *Journal of Marriage and Family* 77, no. 2 (2015): 557–574, https://doi.org/10.1111/jomf.12171; Francine D. Blau, Lawrence M. Kahn, and Kerry L. Papps, "Gender, Source Country Characteristics, and Labor Market Assimilation Among Immigrants," *The Review of Economics and Statistics* 93, no. 1 (2011): 43–58, https://doi.org/10.1162/REST_a_00064.

9 Dawn Marie Dow, *Mothering While Black: Boundaries and Burdens of Middle-Class Parenthood* (University of California Press, 2019).

10 Dow, *Mothering While Black*, 126.

11 Dow, *Mothering While Black*; Joan Williams, *Unbending Gender: Why Family and Work Conflict and What to Do About It* (Oxford University Press, 2001); Andrea Rees Davies and Brenda D. Frink, "The Origins of the Ideal Worker: The Separation of Work and Home in the United States from the Market Revolution to 1950," *Work and Occupations* 41, no. 1 (2014): 18–39, https://doi.org/10.1177 /0730888413515893.

12 Namita N. Manohar, "Gendered Agency in Skilled Migration: The Case of Indian Women in the United States," *Gender & Society* 33, no. 6 (2019): 935–960, https://doi.org/10.1177/0891243219865544.

13 Manohar, "Gendered Agency."

14 Nancy Foner, "Benefits and Burdens: Immigrant Women and Work in New York City," *Gender Issues* 16 (September 1, 1998): 20, https://doi.org/10.1007/s12147-998 -0008-y.

15 Frank and Hou, "Source-Country Gender Roles."

16 Manohar, "Gendered Agency."

17 Emilio A. Parrado and Chenoa Flippen, "Migration and Gender Among Mexican Women," *American Sociological Review* 70 (2005): 606.

Chapter 5   Gendered Work and Work as Independence

1 Evelyn Nakano Glenn, "From Servitude to Service Work: Historical Continuities in the Racial Division of Paid Reproductive Labor," *Signs* 18, no. 1 (1992): 1–43.

2 Enobong Branch, *Opportunity Denied: Limiting Black Women to Devalued Work* (Rutgers University Press, 2011).

3 Mary C. Waters, *Black Identities: West Indian Immigrant Dreams and American Realities* (Russell Sage Foundation; Harvard University Press, 1999).

4 Silvia Pedraza, "Women and Migration: The Social Consequences of Gender," *Annual Review of Sociology* 17 (1991): 303–325.

5 Mary Beth Mills, *Thai Women in the Global Labor Force: Consuming Desires, Contested Selves* (Rutgers University Press, 1999), 11.

6 Aihwa Ong, *Flexible Citizenship: The Cultural Logics of Transnationality* (Duke University Press, 1999), 88.

Chapter 6   All Work Is Cultural Work

1 Yen Le Espiritu, "'We Don't Sleep Around like White Girls Do': Family, Culture, and Gender in Filipina American Lives," *Signs: Journal of Women in Culture and Society* 26, no. 2 (2001): 415–440; George L. Mosse, *Nationalism and Sexuality Respectability and Abnormal Sexuality in Modern Europe* (H. Fertig, 1985); Nira Yuval-Davis, "Women, Citizenship and Difference," *Feminist Review*, no. 57 (1997): 4–27.

2 Carolle Charles, "Gender and Politics in Contemporary Haiti: The Duvalierist State, Transnationalism, and the Emergence of a New Feminism (1980–1990)," *Feminist Studies* 21, no. 1 (1995): 135–164.

3 Régine Latorture, "Haitian Women Underground: Revising Literary Traditions and Societies," *Journal of Haitian Studies*, 5/6 (1999–2000): 80–93; Krista White, "Espousing Ezili: Images of a Lwa, Reflections of the Haitian Woman," *Journal of Haitian Studies* 5/6 (2000): 62–79, https://doi.org/10.7282/T39G5K5W.

4 Bernice Johnson Reagon, "African Diaspora Women: The Making of Cultural Workers," *Feminist Studies* 12, no. 1 (1986): 77.

5 Nina Glick Schiller and Georges E. Fouron, "Terrains of Blood and Nation: Haitian Transnational Social Fields," *Ethnic & Racial Studies* 22, no. 2 (1999): 340–366.

6 Rogers Brubaker, *Citizenship and Nationhood in France and Germany*, vol. 21 (Cambridge University Press, 1992).

7 Nicholas De Genova, "Spectacles of Migrant 'Illegality': The Scene of Exclusion, the Obscene of Inclusion," *Ethnic and Racial Studies* 36, no. 7 (2013): 1180–1198.

8 Schiller and Fouron, "Terrains of Blood and Nation."

Conclusion

1 Aihwa Ong, "Cultural Citizenship as Subject-Making," *Current Anthropology* 37, no. 5 (1996): 737–762.

Afterword

1 David C. Adams and Frances Robles, "Preparations Ramp Up for Global Security Force to Quell Haitian Violence," *New York Times*, May 7, 2024, sec. World, https://www.nytimes.com/2024/05/07/world/africa/haiti-security-force.html.
2 Evens Sanon and Dánica Coto, "UN Human Rights Official Is Alarmed by Sprawling Gang Violence in Haiti," *PBS NewsHour*, October 31, 2023, sec. World, https://www.pbs.org/newshour/world/un-human-rights-official-is-alarmed-by-sprawling-gang-violence-in-haiti.
3 Sanon and Coto, "UN Human Rights Official."

Appendix A

1 There is also a fair amount of Haitian migration to other nations in the Caribbean, Mexico, and South America. While they are outside the scope of this particular study, I am considering looking at those populations in the future.
2 Barney G. Glaser and Anselm L. Strauss, *The Discovery of Grounded Theory: Strategies for Qualitative Research* (Aldine, 1967); John Lofland, *Analyzing Social Settings: A Guide to Qualitative Observation and Analysis*, 4th ed. (Wadsworth/Thomson Learning, 2006).

References

Adams, David C., and Frances Robles. "Preparations Ramp Up for Global Security Force to Quell Haitian Violence." *New York Times*, May 7, 2024, sec. World. https://www.nytimes.com/2024/05/07/world/africa/haiti-security-force.html.

Alba, Richard, and Nancy Foner. "Comparing Immigrant Integration in North America and Western Europe: How Much Do the Grand Narratives Tell Us?" *International Migration Review* 48 (Fall 2014): S263–S291.

Alexander, M. Jacqui. *Pedagogies of Crossing: Meditations on Feminism, Sexual Politics, Memory, and the Sacred*. Duke University Press, 2005.

Althusser, Louis. *For Marx*. Vol. 2. Verso, 1969.

Ameeriar, Lalaie. *Downwardly Global: Women, Work, and Citizenship in the Pakistani Diaspora*. Duke University Press, 2017.

Amrith, Megha, and Nina Sahraoui. *Gender, Work and Migration: Agency in Gendered Labour Settings*. Routledge, 2018.

Arcand, Sébastien, Annick Lenoir-Achdjian, and Denise Helly. "Insertion Professionnelle d'immigrants Récents et Réseaux Sociaux: Le Cas de Maghrébins à Montréal et Sherbrooke." *The Canadian Journal of Sociology / Cahiers Canadiens de Sociologie* 34, no. 2 (2009): 373–402.

Balibar, Etienne. "Racism as Universalism." *New Political Science* 8, no. 1–2 (1989): 9–22.

Basch, Linda G., Nina Glick Schiller, and Cristina Szanton Blanc. *Nations Unbound: Transnational Projects, Postcolonial Predicaments, and Deterritorialized Nation-States*. Gordon and Breach, 2005.

Bastia, Tanja. "Intersectionality, Migration and Development." *Progress in Development Studies* 14, no. 3 (2014): 237–248.

Beaman, Jean. "Citizenship as Cultural: Towards a Theory of Cultural Citizenship." *Sociology Compass* 10, no. 10 (2016): 849–857.

———. *Citizen Outsider: Children of North African Immigrants in France*. University of California Press, 2017.

Benston, Margaret. "The Political Economy of Women's Liberation." *Monthly Review* 41, no. 7 (1989): 31–44.

Bernardin, Renaud. "Le Canada, Le Québec et Haiti." *Le Devoir*, November 7, 1974.

Blad, Cory, and Philippe Couton. "The Rise of an Intercultural Nation: Immigration, Diversity and Nationhood in Quebec." *Journal of Ethnic & Migration Studies* 35, no. 4 (2009): 645–667. https://doi.org/10.1080/13691830902765277.

Blau, Francine D., Lawrence M. Kahn, and Kerry L. Papps. "Gender, Source Country Characteristics, and Labor Market Assimilation Among Immigrants." *The Review of Economics and Statistics* 93, no. 1 (2011): 43–58. https://doi.org/10.1162/REST_a_00064.

Bleich, Erik. "Muslims and the State in the Post-9/11 West: Introduction." *Journal of Ethnic and Migration Studies* 35, no. 3 (2009): 353–360.

———. "On Democratic Integration and Free Speech: Response to Tariq Modood and Randall Hansen." *International Migration* 44, no. 5 (2006): 17–22.

Bloemraad, Irene, Anna Korteweg, and Gökçe Yurdakul. "Citizenship and Immigration: Multiculturalism, Assimilation, and Challenges to the Nation-State." In *Annual Review of Sociology* 34: 153–179. Annual Review of Sociology. Annual Reviews, 2008.

Boudarbat, Brahim, Maude Boulet, and others. "Immigration Au Québec: Politiques et Intégration Au Marché Du Travail." CIRANO, 2010.

Branch, Enobong. *Opportunity Denied: Limiting Black Women to Devalued Work.* Rutgers University Press, 2011.

Brewer, Rose M. "The Radical Black Feminism Project: Rearticulating a Critical Sociology." In *Black Feminist Sociology: Perspectives and Praxis*, edited by Zakiya Luna and Whitney Pirtle. Routledge, 2021.

———. "Theorizing Race, Class and Gender: The New Scholarship of Black Feminist Intellectuals and Black Women's Labor." *Race, Gender & Class* 6, no. 2 (1999): 29–47.

Brown, Karen McCarthy, and Claudine Michel. *Mama Lola: A Vodou Priestess in Brooklyn.* Vol. 4. University of California Press, 2010.

Brown, Tamara Mose. *Raising Brooklyn: Nannies, Childcare, and Caribbeans Creating Community.* New York University Press, 2011.

Brubaker, Rogers. *Citizenship and Nationhood in France and Germany.* Vol. 21. Cambridge University Press, 1992.

Buchanan, Angela B., Nora G. Albert, and Daniel Beaulieu. "The Population with Haitian Ancestry in the United States: 2009." *American Community Survey Briefs.* U.S. Census Bureau, October 2010.

Carbado, Devon W. "Racial Naturalization." *American Quarterly* 57, no. 3 (2005): 633–658.

Carney, Nikita. "All Work Is Cultural Work." *Journal of Haitian Studies* 27, no. 1 (2021): 112–134.

———. "Constructing Race and Ethnicity: 'It Has to Do with Where You Are.'" *Spatial Demography*, June 1, 2021. https://doi.org/10.1007/s40980-021-00087-6.

———. "Multi-Sited Ethnography: Opportunities for the Study of Race." *Sociology Compass* 11, no. 9 (2017).

———. "Race and Ethnicity Across Borders: An Ethnographic Study of Haitian Women in Diaspora." *Issues in Race and Society* 11 (2023): 87–116.

Castañeda, Ernesto. *A Place to Call Home: Immigrant Exclusion and Urban Belonging in New York, Paris, and Barcelona.* Stanford University Press, 2018.

Charles, Carolle. "Gender and Politics in Contemporary Haiti: The Duvalierist State, Transnationalism, and the Emergence of a New Feminism (1980–1990)." *Feminist Studies* 21, no. 1 (1995): 135–164.

Charusheela, S. "Empowering Work? Bargaining Models Reconsidered." In *Toward a Feminist Philosophy of Economics*, edited by Drucilla K. Barker and Edith Kuiper. Routledge, 2003.

Clerge, Orly. *The New Noir: Race, Identity, and Diaspora in Black Suburbia*. University of California Press, 2019.

Coe, Cati. *The New American Servitude: Political Belonging Among African Immigrant Home Care Workers*. New York University Press, 2019.

Cohen, Roger. "Muslim Students' Robes Are Latest Fault Line for French Identity." *New York Times*, September 15, 2023, sec. World. https://www.nytimes.com/2023/09/15/world/europe/france-abaya-ban-attal.html.

Curran, Sara R., Steven Shafer, Katharine M. Donato, and Filiz Garip. "Mapping Gender and Migration in Sociological Scholarship: Is It Segregation or Integration?" *International Migration Review* 40, no. 1 (2006): 199–223.

Davies, Andrea Rees, and Brenda D. Frink. "The Origins of the Ideal Worker: The Separation of Work and Home in the United States from the Market Revolution to 1950." *Work and Occupations* 41, no. 1 (2014): 18–39. https://doi.org/10.1177/0730888413515893.

Dayan, Joan. *Haiti, History, and Gods*. University of California Press, 1995.

De Genova, Nicholas. "Spectacles of Migrant 'Illegality': The Scene of Exclusion, the Obscene of Inclusion." *Ethnic and Racial Studies* 36, no. 7 (2013): 1180–1198.

Del Castillo, Adelaida. "Illegal Status and Social Citizenship: Thoughts on Mexican Immigrants in a Postnational World." In *Women and Migration in the US-Mexico Borderlands: A Reader*, edited by Denise A. Segura and Patricia Zavella. Duke University Press, 2007.

Delachet-Guillon, Claude. *La Communauté Haïtienne En Ile-de-France*. Editions L'Harmattan, 1996.

Donato, Katharine M., Donna Gabaccia, Jennifer Holdaway, Martin Manalansan, and Patricia R. Pessar. "A Glass Half Full? Gender in Migration Studies." *International Migration Review* 40, no. 1 (2006): 3–26.

Dow, Dawn Marie. *Mothering While Black: Boundaries and Burdens of Middle-Class Parenthood*. University of California Press, 2019.

Espiritu, Yen Le. "'We Don't Sleep Around like White Girls Do': Family, Culture, and Gender in Filipina American Lives." *Signs: Journal of Women in Culture and Society* 26, no. 2 (2001): 415–440.

"Étrangers—Immigrés En 2016." L'Institut national de la statistique et des études économiques, 2019. https://www.insee.fr/fr/statistiques/4177162?sommaire=4177618&geo=FE-1.

Faist, Thomas. "Transnationalization in International Migration: Implications for the Study of Citizenship and Culture." *Ethnic and Racial Studies* 23, no. 2 (2000): 189–222.

Faist, Thomas, Margit Fauser, and Eveline Reisenauer. *Transnational Migration*. Polity, 2013.

Fanon, Frantz. *Black Skin, White Masks*. Grove, 1952.

Favell, Adrian. *Philosophies of Integration: Immigration and the Idea of Citizenship in France and Britain*. Springer, 2016.

Flores, Juan. "'Que Assimilated, Brother, Yo Soy Asimilao': The Structuring of Puerto Rican Identity in the US." *The Journal of Ethnic Studies* 13, no. 3 (1985): 1–16.

Foner, Nancy. "Benefits and Burdens: Immigrant Women and Work in New York City." *Gender Issues* 16 (September 1, 1998): 5–24. https://doi.org/10.1007/s12147-998-0008-y.

———. "Gender and Migration: West Indians in Comparative Perspective." *International Migration* 47, no. 1 (2009): 3–29.

Formisano, Ronald P. *Boston Against Busing: Race, Class, and Ethnicity in the 1960s and 1970s*. University of North Carolina Press, 2004.

Foucault, Michel. *Discipline and Punish: The Birth of the Prison*. Vintage Books, 1979.

Fouron, Georges, and Nina Glick Schiller. "All in the Family: Gender, Transnational Migration, and the Nation-State." *Identities: Global Studies in Culture and Power* 7, no. 4 (2001): 539–582.

Frank, Kristyn, and Feng Hou. "Source-Country Gender Roles and the Division of Labor Within Immigrant Families." *Journal of Marriage and Family* 77, no. 2 (2015): 557–574. https://doi.org/10.1111/jomf.12171.

Freedman, Jane. *Immigration and Insecurity in France*. Routledge, 2017. https://doi.org/10.4324/9781315252582.

Gálvez, Alyshia. "Immigrant Citizenship: Neoliberalism, Immobility and the Vernacular Meanings of Citizenship." *Identities* 20, no. 6 (2013): 720–737.

Gauthier, Carol-Anne. "Obstacles to Socioeconomic Integration of Highly-Skilled Immigrant Women: Lessons from Quebec Interculturalism and Implications for Diversity Management." Edited by Charlotte Holgersson, Irene Ryan, and Inge Bleijenbergh. *Equality, Diversity and Inclusion: An International Journal* 35, no. 1 (2016): 17–30. https://doi.org/10.1108/EDI-03-2014-0022.

Geertz, Clifford. "Thick Description: Toward an Interpretive Theory of Culture." In *Readings in the Philosophy of Social Science*, edited by Michael Martin and Lee C. McIntyre. MIT Press, 1994.

Germain, Félix F. "Caribbean Women in Postwar France, 1946–1974." In *Decolonizing the Republic: African and Caribbean Migrants in Postwar Paris, 1946–1974*. Ruth Simms Hamilton African Diaspora. Michigan State University Press, 2016. http://www.jstor.org/stable/10.14321/j.ctt1bkm6rf.10.

Gilroy, Paul. *The Black Atlantic: Modernity and Double Consciousness*. Harvard University Press, 1993.

Glaser, Barney G., and Anselm L. Strauss. *The Discovery of Grounded Theory: Strategies for Qualitative Research*. Aldine, 1967.

Glenn, Evelyn Nakano. "From Servitude to Service Work: Historical Continuities in the Racial Division of Paid Reproductive Labor." *Signs* 18, no. 1 (1992): 1–43.

Government of Canada, Statistics Canada. "Census Profile, 2016 Census—Montréal, Ville [Census Subdivision], Quebec and Quebec [Province]," February 8, 2017. https://www12.statcan.gc.ca/census-recensement/2016/dp-pd/prof/details/page.cfm?Lang=E&Geo1=CSD&Code1=2466023&Geo2=PR&Code2=24&SearchText=Montreal&SearchType=Begins&SearchPR=01&B1=Ethnic%20origin&TABID=1&type=0.

Hall, Stuart. "Race, Articulation, and Societies Structured in Dominance." In *Black British Cultural Studies: A Reader*, edited by Houston A. Baker, Jr., Manthia Diawara, and Ruth H. Lindeborg. University of Chicago Press, 1996.

Handlin, Oscar. *Boston's Immigrants, 1790–1880: A Study in Acculturation*. Harvard University Press, 1991.

Hargreaves, Alec G. *Multi-Ethnic France: Immigration, Politics, Culture and Society*. 2nd ed. Routledge, 2007.

Herrera, Gioconda. "Gender and International Migration: Contributions and Cross-Fertilizations." *Annual Review of Sociology* 39 (2013): 471–489.

Hikido, Annie. "Entrepreneurship in South African Township Tourism: The Impact of Interracial Social Capital." *Ethnic and Racial Studies* 41, no. 14 (2018): 2580–2598.

Hondagneu-Sotelo, Pierrette. *Gender and U.S. Immigration: Contemporary Trends.* University of California Press, 2003. Table of Contents. http://www.loc.gov/catdir /toc/fy038/2002043198.html.

Hunter, Margaret. "The Persistent Problem of Colorism: Skin Tone, Status, and Inequality." *Sociology Compass* 1, no. 1 (2007): 237–254. https://doi.org/10.1111/j .1751-9020.2007.00006.x.

Itzigsohn, José. "Immigration and the Boundaries of Citizenship: The Institutions of Immigrants' Political Transnationalism." *International Migration Review* 34, no. 4 (2000): 1126–1154.

Jackson, Regine O., ed. *Geographies of the Haitian Diaspora.* Routledge, 2011.

Jadotte, Herard. "Haitian Immigration to Quebec." *Journal of Black Studies* 7, no. 4 (1977): 485–500.

James, Erica Caple. *Democratic Insecurities: Violence, Trauma, and Intervention in Haiti.* University of California Press, 2010.

Johnson, Marilynn S. *The New Bostonians: How Immigrants Have Transformed the Metro Area Since the 1960s.* University of Massachusetts Press, 2015.

Joppke, Christian. "Multiculturalism and Immigration: A Comparison of the United States, Germany, and Great Britain." *Theory and Society* 25, no. 4 (1996): 449–500.

Kim, Marlene. "Race and Ethnicity in the Workplace." In *Handbook of Research on Gender and Economic Life*, edited by Deborah M. Figart and Tonia L. Warnecke. Edward Elgar, 2013.

Kostov, Chris. "Canada-Quebec Immigration Agreements (1971–1991) and Their Impact on Federalism." *American Review of Canadian Studies* 38, no. 1 (2008): 91–103. https://doi.org/10.1080/02722010809481822.

Labelle, Micheline. *Idéologie de Couleur et Classes Sociales En Haïti.* Presses de l'Université de Montréal, 1987. http://classiques.uqac.ca/contemporains/labelle _micheline/ideologie_de_couleur_en_haiti/labelle_ideologie_couleur.pdf?

Labelle, Micheline, Serge Larose, and Victor Piché. "Émigration et immigration: Les Haïtiens au Québec." *Sociologie et sociétés* 15, no. 2 (1983): 73–88. https://doi.org/10 .7202/001394ar.

Labelle, Micheline, and François Rocher. "Immigration, Integration and Citizenship Policies in Canada and Quebec." In *Immigration and Self-Government of Minority Nations.* Peter Lang, 2009.

Laguerre, Michel S. *Diasporic Citizenship: Haitian Americans in Transnational America.* St. Martin's, 1998.

Lamphere, Louise, Alex Stepick, and Guillermo J. Grenier. *Newcomers in the Workplace: Immigrants and the Restructing of the US Economy.* Temple University Press, 1994.

Latorture, Régine. "Haitian Women Underground: Revising Literary Traditions and Societies." *Journal of Haitian Studies* 5/6 (1999–2000): 80–93.

Leca, Jean. "Questions on Citizenship." In *Dimensions of Radical Democracy: Pluralism, Citizenship, Community*, edited by Chantal Mouffe. Verso, 1992.

Levin, Andrew. "Civil Society and Democratization in Haiti." *Emory International Law Review* 9, no. 2 (1995): 389–458

Levitt, Peggy, and B. Nadya Jaworsky. "Transnational Migration Studies: Past Developments and Future Trends." *Annual Review of Sociology* 33 (2007): 129–156.

Linstroth, J. P., Alison Hall, Mamyrah A. Douge-Prosper, and Patrick T. Hiller. "Conflicting Ambivalence of Haitian Identity-Making in South Florida." *Forum: Qualitative Social Research* 10, no. 3 (2009): 1–37.

Lofland, John. *Analyzing Social Settings: A Guide to Qualitative Observation and Analysis*. 4th ed. Wadsworth/Thomson Learning, 2006.

Lowe, Lisa. *Immigrant Acts: On Asian American Cultural Politics*. Duke University Press, 1996.

Lupo, Alan. *Liberty's Chosen Home: The Politics of Violence in Boston*. Beacon, 1988.

Lutz, Helma. "Gender in the Migratory Process." *Journal of Ethnic & Migration Studies* 36, no. 10 (2010): 1647–1663.

Mahler, Sarah J., and Patricia R. Pessar. "Gender Matters: Ethnographers Bring Gender from the Periphery Toward the Core of Migration Studies." *International Migration Review* 40, no. 1 (2006): 27–63.

Manohar, Namita N. "Gendered Agency in Skilled Migration: The Case of Indian Women in the United States." *Gender & Society* 33, no. 6 (2019): 935–960. https://doi.org/10.1177/0891243219865544.

Marable, Manning. *How Capitalism Underdeveloped Black America: Problems in Race, Political Economy, and Society*. Haymarket Books, 2015.

Marcelin, Louis Herns. "Identity, Power, and Socioracial Hierarchies Among Haitian Immigrants in Florida." In *Neither Enemies nor Friends: Latinos, Blacks, Afro-Latinos*, edited by Anani Dzidzienyo and Suzanne Oboler. Palgrave Macmillan, 2005. Table of Contents. http://www.loc.gov/catdir/toc/hol052/2004052797.html.

Margolis, Maxine L. "From Mistress to Servant: Downward Mobility Among Brazilian Immigrants in New York City." *Urban Anthropology and Studies of Cultural Systems and World Economic Development* 19, no. 3 (1990): 215–231.

Marshall, T. H. (Thomas Humphrey). *Class, Citizenship, and Social Development: Essays*. Anchor Books, 1965.

McAlister, Elizabeth. "Sacred Stories from the Haitian Diaspora: A Collective Biography of Seven Vodou Priestesses in New York City." *Journal of Caribbean Studies* 9, no. 1 & 2 (1993).: 10–27

Menino, Thomas M. "Imagine All the People: Haitian Immigrants in Boston." New Bostonian Series. City of Boston, June 2009.

Miller, Toby. *Cultural Citizenship: Cosmopolitanism, Consumerism, and Television in a Neoliberal Age*. Temple University Press, 2007.

Mills, Mary Beth. *Thai Women in the Global Labor Force: Consuming Desires, Contested Selves*. Rutgers University Press, 1999.

Mills, Sean. "Quebec, Haiti, and the Deportation Crisis of 1974." *The Canadian Historical Review* 94, no. 3 (2013): 405–435.

Modood, Tariq, and Pnina Werbner. *The Politics of Multiculturalism in the New Europe: Racism, Identity, and Community*. Zed Books, 1997.

Mollard, Blandine, and Sanober Umar. "Gender, Migration and Deskilling: A Broad Review of the Literature." In *Crushed Hopes: Underemployment and Deskilling Among Skilled Migrant Women*. International Organization for Migration, 2013, 9–36.

Mosse, George L. *Nationalism and Sexuality Respectability and Abnormal Sexuality in Modern Europe*. H. Fertig, 1985.

O'Connor, Thomas H. *The Boston Irish: A Political History*. Northeastern University Press, 1995.

Ong, Aihwa. "Cultural Citizenship as Subject-Making." *Current Anthropology* 37, no. 5 (1996): 737–762.

———. *Flexible Citizenship: The Cultural Logics of Transnationality*. Duke University Press, 1999.

———. *Spirits of Resistance and Capitalist Discipline: Factory Women in Malaysia.* State University of New York Press, 2010.

Orozco, Manuel, and Elisabeth Burgess. "A Commitment Amidst Shared Hardship: Haitian Transnational Migrants and Remittances." *Journal of Black Studies* 42, no. 2 (2011): 225–246.

Parrado, Emilio A., and Chenoa Flippen. "Migration and Gender Among Mexican Women." *American Sociological Review* 70 (2005): 606–632.

Parreñas, Rhacel Salazar. *Servants of Globalization: Migration and Domestic Work.* Stanford University Press, 2015.

Pedraza, Silvia. "Women and Migration: The Social Consequences of Gender." *Annual Review of Sociology* 17 (1991): 303–325.

Pegram, Scooter. "Being Ourselves: Immigrant Culture and Self-Identification Among Young Haitians in Montréal." *Ethnic Studies Review* 28 (2005): 1–20.

Pessar, Patricia R. "Engendering Migration Studies: The Case of New Immigrants in the United States." In *Gender and U.S. Immigration: Contemporary Trends*, edited by Pierrette Hondagneu-Sotelo. University of California Press, 2003. http://www .jstor.org/stable/10.1525/j.ctt1pntog.5.

Pessar, Patricia R., and Sarah J. Mahler. "Transnational Migration: Bringing Gender In." *International Migration Review* 37, no. 3 (2003): 812–846.

Pierre-Louis, François. "Haitian Immigrants and the Greater Caribbean Community of New York City: Challenges and Opportunities." *Memorias: Revista Digital de Historia y Arqueología Desde El Caribe* 10, no. 21 (2013): 22–40.

Reagon, Bernice Johnson. "African Diaspora Women: The Making of Cultural Workers." *Feminist Studies* 12, no. 1 (1986): 77–90.

Reitz, Jeffrey G. "Immigrant Employment Success in Canada, Part I: Individual and Contextual Causes." *Journal of International Migration and Integration / Revue de l'integration et de La Migration Internationale* 8, no. 1 (2007): 11–36. https://doi .org/10.1007/s12134-007-0001-4.

———. "Immigrant Employment Success in Canada, Part II: Understanding the Decline." *Journal of International Migration and Integration / Revue de l'integration et de La Migration Internationale* 8, no. 1 (2007): 37–62. https://doi .org/10.1007/s12134-007-0002-3.

Roder, Iannis. "Abaya Ban in French Schools: 'Wearing the Abaya Is a Political Gesture.'" *Le Monde.Fr*, September 9, 2023. https://www.lemonde.fr/en/opinion /article/2023/09/09/france-s-abaya-ban-wearing-the-abaya-is-a-political-gesture _6131329_23.html.

Rosaldo, Renato. "Cultural Citizenship and Educational Democracy." *Cultural Anthropology* 9, no. 3 (1994): 402–411.

———. "Cultural Citizenship, Inequality, and Multiculturalism." In *Race, Identity, and Citizenship: A Reader*, edited by Rodolfo D. Torres, Louis F. Mirón, and Jonathan X. Inda. Blackwell, 1999.

Ruggles, Steven, Sarah Flood, Ronald Goeken, Josiah Grover, Erin Meyer, Jose Pacas, and Matthew Sobek. "IPUMS USA: Version 10.0 [Dataset]." IPUMS, 2020. https://doi.org/10.18128/D010.V10.0.

Sanon, Evens, and Dánica Coto. "UN Human Rights Official Is Alarmed by Sprawling Gang Violence in Haiti." *PBS NewsHour*, October 31, 2023, sec. World. https://www.pbs.org/newshour/world/un-human-rights-official-is-alarmed-by -sprawling-gang-violence-in-haiti.

Schiller, Nina Glick, Josh DeWind, Marie Lucie Brutus, Carolle Charles, Georges Fouron, and Antoine Thomas. "All in the Same Boat? Unity and Diversity in Haitian Organizing in New York." *Center for Migration Studies Special Issues* 7, no. 1 (1989): 167–184.

Schiller, Nina Glick, and Georges Eugene Fouron. *Georges Woke up Laughing: Long-Distance Nationalism and the Search for Home*. Duke University Press, 2001.

———. "Terrains of Blood and Nation: Haitian Transnational Social Fields." *Ethnic & Racial Studies* 22, no. 2 (1999): 340–366.

Schmidt, Hans. *The United States Occupation of Haiti, 1915–1934*. Rutgers University Press, 1995.

Schuller, Mark. "Participation, More than Add Women and Stir? A Comparative Case Analysis in Post-Coup Haiti." *Caribbean Review of Gender Studies* 2 (2008): 1–34.

Scott, Joan Wallach. *The Politics of the Veil*. Princeton University Press, 2009.

Shoaff, Jennifer L. "Haitian Migrant Women, Dominican Pepeceras, and the Power Geographies of Transnational Markets." In *Transatlantic Feminisms: Women and Gender Studies in Africa and the Diaspora*, edited by Cheryl R. Rodriguez et al. Lexington Books, 2015.

Smith, Michael Peter, and Luis Eduardo Guarnizo, eds. *Transnationalism from Below*. Vol. 6. Transaction Publishers, 1998.

Stack, John F, Jr. *International Conflict in an American City: Boston's Irish, Italians, and Jews, 1935–1944*. Greenwood, 1979.

Stevenson, Nick. "Cultural Citizenship in the 'Cultural' Society: A Cosmopolitan Approach." *Citizenship Studies* 7, no. 3 (2003): 331–348.

Stoler, Ann Laura. *Carnal Knowledge and Imperial Power: Race and the Intimate in Colonial Rule*. University of California Press, 2010.

Trouillot, Michel-Rolph. *Silencing the Past: Power and the Production of History*. Beacon, 1995.

U.S. Census Bureau. "American Community Survey," 2021. https://data.census.gov /table?q=haitians+demographics&t=581&tid=ACSSPP1Y2021.S0201.

Voas, David, and Fenella Fleischmann. "Islam Moves West: Religious Change in the First and Second Generations." *Annual Review of Sociology* 38, no. 1 (2012): 525–545.

Vrabel, Jim. *A People's History of the New Boston*. University of Massachusetts Press, 2014. http://www.jstor.org/stable/j.ctt5vk3fs.

Waters, Mary C. *Black Identities: West Indian Immigrant Dreams and American Realities*. Russell Sage Foundation; Harvard University Press, 1999.

———. "West Indians and African Americans at Work: Structural Differences and Cultural Stereotypes." In *Immigration and Opportunity: Race, Ethnicity, and Employment in the United States*, edited by Stephanie Bell-Rose and Frank D. Bean. Russell Sage Foundation, 2003. http://muse.jhu.edu/book/42175.

White, Krista. "Espousing Ezili: Images of a Lwa, Reflections of the Haitian Woman." *Journal of Haitian Studies* 5/6 (2000): 62–79. https://doi.org/10.7282/T39G5K5W.

Williams, Joan. *Unbending Gender: Why Family and Work Conflict and What to Do About It*. Oxford University Press, 2001.

Wingfield, Adia Harvey. *Flatlining: Race, Work, and Health Care in the New Economy*. University of California Press, 2019.

Yuval-Davis, Nira. "Women, Citizenship and Difference." *Feminist Review*, no. 57 (1997): 4–27.

Index

About the Author

NIKITA CARNEY is an assistant professor of sociology at Bentley University. She focuses her research and teaching on issues of race, gender, and culture. Her work is published in journals such as the *Annual Review of Sociology, Social Currents*, and the *Journal of Haitian Studies*.